THE BUSINESS OF MUSIC

PROFIT
FROM YOUR
MUSIC

James Gibson

Omnibus Press
London/Sydney

*To Sandra, Chris, Laura
and my parents . . . music
lovers all*

First published by Writers Digest Books, Cincinnati, Ohio, USA

© 1986 James Gibson
This edition © Copyright 1990 Omnibus Press
(A Division of Book Sales Limited)

Edited by Chris Barstow

Cover designed by Pearce Marchbank

Cover photo by Julian Hawkins

Text art direction by AB3

ISBN 0.7119.1716.7

Order No: OP 45137

All rights reserved. No part of this book may be reproduced in any form or by any electronic or mechanical means, including information storage or retrieval systems, without permission in writing from the publisher, except by a reviewer who may quote brief passages.

Exclusive distributors:
Book Sales Limited,
8/9 Frith Street,
London W1V 5TZ, UK.

Music Sales Pty Limited,
120 Rothschild Avenue,
Rosebery, NSW 2018, Australia.

To the Music Trade only:
Music Sales Limited,
8/9 Frith Street,
London W1V 5TZ, UK.

Typeset by Wakeworth
Printed in England by
St. Edmundsbury Press,
Bury St. Edmunds, Suffolk.

CONTENTS

Know when you're ready by visiting jobs you'd like to be playing. Notice styles, ask questions, learn the repertoire, polish your showmanship. Use home audio-visual equipment to fine-tune your performance skills. Learn from the pros, maybe as an apprentice. Know what the job really is, and make sure you measure up.

You can make a steady, high-paying career out of one-night stands if the stands are in good places and the nights are close enough together. You need to know the conditions in your musical field and decide whether you'd do better to organise a new group or join one that's already established. Maybe you should do both, *and* become a musical contractor, *and* solo on the side. For that, you'll need a job-finding system.

Start out facing the facts of the marketplace. Clients expect to get what they pay for, not just what you happen to like. But every profession has its trade-offs, and doing what *they* like can support you in doing what *you* like. Besides musical satisfactions, you'll learn the satisfaction of 'a professional job well done.' The bottom line is always finding enough people who like your music enough to pay for it.

A successful musician is a salesman, an advertising specialist, a secretary, an accountant, a stage manager, a sound engineer, an equipment mover, and much more besides. You need to build up contacts and learn to 'network' – in person, by phone, and by post – not wait for the jobs to come beating on your door. Learn to do the paperwork that will keep your career rolling along, and present a professional appearance in all your operations

Keep out of the ruts that can kill your love of music, but stay interested (and financially stable) by scheduling a variety of jobs that will help keep your enjoyment and your musicianship fresh.

in you the creativity and flexibility necessary to keep up with the changes in your community and keep your love of music alive.

PREFACE

Susan Bennett, a housewife and mother, has a great part-time job. It's easy, fun and profitable. Most weeks, she makes a hundred pounds or more for just a few hours of work

Her job? She sings with a freelance dance band. "It's great," she says, "to get out of the household routine, have fun making music, *and* get paid for it."

Allen Stone is a computer programmer for a large company. Many weeks he makes as much money in a few nights, by playing bass with a pop-rock band, as he does in a week on his regular job. Furthermore, he usually works only three or four hours a night.

Brenda Malone is a harpist who plays mostly classical music. She teaches part time in a local school, has a few private students, plays several nights every week in an elegant restaurant and frequently performs for private parties and receptions. She makes a good living from her full-time musical career, though she doesn't have a 'regular' job, and she enjoys the variety and stimulation of working in different settings.

Susan, Allen and Brenda are profiting from the freelance music marketplace. Like thousands of other performers, they work an interesting variety of jobs and make a substantial income from their music.

On an hourly basis, in fact, their incomes often rival those of lawyers, accountants and other professionals. And, since they enjoy music, it's like getting paid for having fun.

Could you make money with music? Did you play an instrument at school or college? Do you play in a part-time, amateur band or sing with a barbershop quartet? Do you enjoy playing the piano or guitar to entertain your friends?

Or are you now a professional musician but not getting enough jobs, not making enough money? Are you caught in the routine world of clubs and hotels bored with your music – and depressed by your bank statement? Would you like to broaden your musical market to include some of the high-paying jobs that have eluded you?

This book will show you how to make money – or more money – from your music.

Most people think of nightclubs, concerts or records as the main sources of income for professional musicians. But this is a very limited view, for there are *hundreds of ways* to profit from your music. Many of these opportunities are one-time or part-time events that need freelance musicians who are alert, capable and available.

Many of the best freelance jobs involve playing for private gatherings that the public never hears about. How do you find such jobs? That's where this book comes in. It discusses nearly a hundred different places to sell your music, and it gives you a system for finding the right jobs for you.

Susan and Allen, as part-time musicians, and Brenda, even as a full-time player aren't tied down to steady musical jobs. They have plenty of free time, and their incomes rival those of professionals in other fields. These three successful musicians have learned how to market their music to get the maximum pay for the minimum time.

You can do the same.

INTRODUCTION

WHY YOU NEED
THIS BOOK

All freelance musicians ask the same question: how can I find more work and make more money?

That question never goes away. Beginners and established professionals alike seek the answer every day. The answer is really quite simple: play more jobs, and you'll make more money.

But are there really jobs that need your music?

Yes – *if you know where they are*. And if you know how to secure and play these low-visibility, high-profit engagements, you'll maximise your profits. The hardest part is finding jobs that need your music.

Profit From Your Music offers a universally applicable system for finding jobs. This book will show you how to establish contact with the very people who *need* your music and will pay for it. You'll learn about hundreds of different markets, and you'll discover how to pinpoint those that need *your* particular talents.

This system isn't limited to one kind of music or to one category of musicians. It will work for practically every freelance musician, although each player's approach will differ, depending on his or her own desires, experience and talent.

Success in playing music for a living doesn't have to be a matter of luck or of who you know. *Profit From Your Music* presents a clear method that – step by step – will help you find more work.

How This Book is Arranged You will find several kinds of help in *Profit From Your Music*. First we'll discuss the general philosophy of freelance music, of selling creativity for money. There are a few crucial ideas here that will help ensure your success. Second, we'll get to the practical aspects of the profession. We'll talk about getting organised and becoming business-like. Then you'll learn how to assess your talents methodically, and use some simple market-research techniques to match those talents to the markets you will discover. The jobs you find with this method will be *yours alone*, targeted to your own abilities and aspirations. Worksheets are provided for you to use in preparing your own marketing plan.

The main focus is on *finding jobs*, and the mechanism you'll use is called the *Personal Music Marketing System*, or *PMMS*. Devising your own marketing system will require a little work, but it will be well worth it. If you don't use such a system in today's competitive music market, you'll waste countless hours and lots of effort. *Profit From Your Music* will show you how to plan your time and how to focus your energy most effectively. Then you'll learn how to use the market information you've developed to locate and meet potential clients, convince them to hire you, and book and play the job.

Even If You're a Genius

Why should a musician have to use a handbook like this to find jobs? Won't agents or band-leaders do that for you? Won't clients call if they need you?

No, they won't.

There are too many musicians and too few jobs for us to relax for long. Even if you are a certified genius, a child prodigy with perfect pitch and a photographic memory, you'll still have to scramble for jobs.

Profit From Your Music shows you a new way to think about yourself and your music – an approach that will help you locate, book and play jobs that need you.

One main point can be stated simply. Playing the job is easy. Finding the job is difficult. That's where this book comes in; it's a marketing guide.

So you won't find any music in this book – not a single note. You should already know how to play your instrument – or be working on it. The book assumes that you are a competent musician, capable of making good music.

If you need to work on your musical technique, this may not be the book for you – yet. But there are thousands of instructional methods, courses and books that will help you improve your playing.

What about Fame and Fortune?

Would you like to be on the cover of glossy magazines? How about being featured on TV?

Let's be honest right at the beginning. This book isn't intended to make you rich and famous. We make no claims that it can make you a star, or a wealthy recording artist, or a fixture of the concert circuit.

Becoming a celebrity is, for some people, a worthwhile goal. If that's your desire, work for it. But remember, becoming a star depends on many factors, most of which are out of your control. Hard work and talent will surely be necessary, but so will good luck, charisma, a healthy economy – and knowing the right people.

So if you want to be a superstar, by all means read the books, including the ones by fabulously rich celebrities, that purport to show you how to become famous, pick the right manager, agent, road crew, lawyer and recording company. But realise that only a tiny fraction of those who read such books will ever really profit from their from-the-top advice.

Fewer than one percent of all working musicians ever become household names. That leaves more than 99 percent of us to make our living from music in our own communities.

Profit From Your Music will show you how to prosper by working more frequently in your community, playing music that you enjoy. If this leads to recording contracts and concert dates, that's great! Most working musicians, however, will never attain fame or fortune. Many don't want to.

Making a good living playing music that you, your client and your audience enjoy is an enviable – and achievable – goal. Millions of people go to work each day hating every minute of it, and you have a chance to get paid for doing what you like best.

Part-Time and Full-Time

This book is for *all* musicians who want to profit – or profit more – from music. That includes full-time professionals and part-time players. Most of the emphasis here, however, is on the harder-to-find part-time freelance jobs. Since most of these jobs aren't performed for the public, they aren't easy to locate and book.

Many of these one-time jobs, however, are the cream of the freelance music world. On an hourly basis, these are among the best-paying opportunities for working musicians.

These engagements exist in virtually every part of the country, and if you really want to maximise your musical income, you'll try to play as many of these jobs as you can.

Of course, we also discuss full-time work for freelance musicians. Restaurants, clubs, and such steady employment as teaching, working in shops, and playing with symphony orchestras provide lots of opportunity. But the musical spectrum is much broader than these common opportunities, and our method teaches you to search out the little-known freelance jobs that can increase your income or support your entire musical career.

So, if you're a computer programmer who moonlights as a jazz keyboardist, or a landscape gardener who plays the fiddle in a part-time folk band, this book will help you find new places to sell your music. And if you are in a covers band that plays six nights a week in local clubs, you'll find many suggestions here for other well-paying outlets for your music so you can earn even more.

It doesn't matter whether you play full-time for a living or use music as a part-time – but well-paying – hobby. What does matter is your ability to find jobs that will pay you to perform. Your goal is to fill your diary with high-quality jobs that will pay you for doing what you like best – making music. This book will show you how.

CHAPTER ONE

ARE
YOU GOOD
ENOUGH?

How good must you be to make money with your music? Perfect? Average? Fair? This is a difficult, but important, question that each musician must answer.

Your musical skills should never stop growing. Like a doctor or lawyer, you practise your profession. As music changes, you have to keep up; you can never relax and assume that you're as good as you should be. No one ever is.

How to Tell if You're Ready to Make Money with Your Music

Visiting jobs you'd like to be playing. Listen and watch to learn what is involved. Which styles should you know? What tunes seem to be the essential 'core repertoire' in that style? Are the other musicians reading music? Could you rely on a fake book (which provides only melody lines and chord symbols), or must you know the music without having charts to work from?

Ask questions. Talk to people who play the kind of engagement you are interested in, and get first-hand reports on what is required. Many musical jobs seem more intimidating at first than they really are.

Study the repertoire. If you're going after a job playing classical guitar in an exclusive restaurant, do you know enough music to play for three or four hours without repeating? Do you know the numbers that are likely to be requested?

Polish your showmanship. If you want to sing with a dance or covers band, do you know enough lyrics? Do you know how to work a microphone and relate to the crowd? Is your pitch good? Do you understand the structure of melodies, so you will know when to sing and when to leave space for an instrumental solo? Can you do the same song several times a night, night after night, without getting bored (or letting your boredom show)?

Learn specialised repertoires. If your target is booking enthnic wedding receptions, are you familiar with all the necessary tunes and tempos? Do you know the music for horas, polkas, tarantellas, merengues, or whatever kind of music the client may want?

Nobody is born knowing all this, but you can learn what you need for the jobs you want to play.

High-Tech Learning

Use home audiovisual equipment as a learning tool. Borrow or hire what you don't have. Tape record your playing or singing, and listen critically. Don't be over-sensitive when you hear yourself, but listen objectively for the most important elements of your performance.

If you're a singer, listen to your pitch and phrasing. If you're a drummer, use a metronome to assess your time-keeping – from a performance tape, not a practice session. Flashy solos and the best musical equipment won't help if you rush or drag badly.

Use a video camera to find out how you look, particularly if you're a singer or need to be involved with the audience. A few video sessions will clearly reveal any amateurish flaws.

One good way to improve your playing, learn new tunes, and have the chance to play with top professionals is to use play-along records. Such popular series as Music Minus One and the Jamie Abersold records offer valuable experience at modest cost. If you can't play 'Stardust' or 'Body and Soul,' you'll have a hard time establishing yourself as a capable big-band player, but play-along records can teach you these standard tunes and prepare you well for playing for money.

Again, nobody's perfect. Keep your perspective by remembering how most pop records are made. Days – or weeks – of overdubbing, adding tracks, and 'punching in' to cover mistakes ensure that every recording will be flawless. Even classical piano albums have been pieced together from several recording sessions to get the best possible performance. It's not fair to judge your live performance against the contrived perfection of most albums.

Learning From Others

There are all kinds of music teachers, and they can be of great value to both beginning and advanced musicians. You'll learn more and save much time if you work with a good teacher.

But finding the right teacher to prepare you for playing *professionally* can be difficult. Learning traditional music and proper technique may not be enough. You may require a teacher who understands your special needs and who can provide comprehensive guidance in the most effective sequence. How do you go about finding someone to help you acquire the skills you need?

First, define exactly what you want to learn. If you simply want to work on technique, or reading, or some standard aspect of your instrument, you'll probably be able to find plenty of capable teachers. If, however, you want to learn current pop styles, jazz improvisation, or computer/synthesiser/programming, you'll have a smaller selection of experts who can assist you.

That goes especially for improvisation. In many non-classical job situations, the ability to improvise is of the utmost importance, yet it's a very difficult – if not impossible – skill to teach. Many excellent improvisers, for example, just 'play naturally,' and can't tell anyone else how to do it.

Often, you will profit by taking lessons from a professional player who is not primarily a teacher. Here, though, you must be sure that that player knows how to teach and can communicate well. Talk to the best players in your area to get leads on appropriate teachers, and investigate institutions devoted to your kind of music.

It is certainly possible to become a master musician all by yourself, but why continue to invent the wheel? Use the experience and specialised knowledge of other musicians to save yourself time and effort. Just be sure that the teacher you choose is the teacher you need.

Again, music is practised. It's not mastered once and for all. If you're good enough today, you may not be adequate tomorrow unless you continue to work at it. Musicians at the very highest levels always continue to practise and work, and you should too.

Knowing What's Needed

But exactly how good is good enough for commerical music? These points will help you answer that question:

- Be sure you're good enough to do the job. If you have doubts about your ability, don't take the engagement! A poor performance will be long remembered by clients, the audience and other musicians. If you don't think you can perform at a professional level, don't try. You could do more harm than good, and the money you make just won't be worth the damage to your career.
- On the other hand don't wait to practise until you're perfect, or you'll never leave your house. There will always be room for improvement – current tunes to learn, more styles to acquire, or new equipment to master.
- Don't overlook the non-musical factors that are crucial to freelance success. Sometimes, a business-like attitude and pleasant personality are as important as your playing ability. Even marvellous musicians usually have to be on time and be able to get along with the band, the client and the audience.
- Knowing what the job requires is also important. How will the music fit the overall plan of the event? What's the larger perspective? What, really, is needed from the musicians? Virtuosity? Usually not. For most jobs, competent playing will be enough.
- Finally, since you're a musician, you will usually be a harsher critic of your playing than your clients will be. As long as you can provide what they need, you're good enough for the job.

CHAPTER TWO

WHY
YOU NEED A
JOB-FINDING
SYSTEM

Freelance musicians work on a job-by-job basis, and often have no steady employment. They play shows, one-off gigs, and a wide range of miscellaneous engagements. Some work five or six nights a week in restaurants or clubs, while others don't want such regular work.

They are part-timers or full-time professionals. They may be teachers, students, carpenters, airline pilots, or orchestral players. At one time or another, almost all musicians take freelance jobs, sometimes for extra money, or to survive between steady engagements, or as professional, full-time freelancers.

Freelancing can be financially dangerous because there is no steady income. But it can also be exciting, with new challenges each day. And many full-time freelancers make an excellent living without ever having a steady job.

But we all face the same problem. Finding work. No matter how good you are or how long you've been a professional, you will have to find clients who are willing to pay you money to perform.

How Bad Is It Each year there are more and more events and celebrations that need music. But competition keeps pace. There are already far more players than there are regular salaried jobs, and the musician-to-job ratio gets worse all the time.

Precise figures are hard to find, but the staggering increase in the amount of money spent on music and instruments over the last 25 years indicates how many people are interested in professional music. Indeed, interest in music, both amateur and professional, is growing faster than the nation's economy.

You might conclude from this that only the most talented are likely to find regular employment. But in most cases, it takes more than just talent to succeed.

Classical Music: Too Much Talent Too Few Jobs Established symphony orchestras and opera companies can absorb only a few new classical players and singers each year. Since most orchestral players are very career-minded, and since these jobs are difficult to find in the first place, turnover in this area of music is very low.

Nevertheless, music colleges, universities, conservatories and private teachers, continue to produce thousands of classical musicians each year.

The question is obvious. Where are all of these excellently trained musicians to work? How can they make money with their music if there are so few full-time jobs?

For Pop Music It's Even Worse Pop, jazz, country and rock music attract untold thousands of new performers each year. Since anyone can call her or himself a professional, and play for pay, there is no way to know how many part-time musicians there are. However, we all know from experience that the number far exceeds the number of jobs available.

What can freelance musicians do? What steps are necessary to prosper – or even survive?

The job-finding system explained in this book will help you match your talents to jobs that need you, whether you're a classical violinist or a country fiddler. Freelance success requires playing many jobs, and this method is an organised approach that will help you target, book and play engagements that are right for you.

To be successful, you must be prepared.

Leader or Sideman? Should you organise your own musical group and take the responsibility of being a *leader?* Or should you try only to work for other musicians?

You should probably do both. If you are to profit as a freelance musician, you'll have to work as much as possible. Sometimes this may be as a leader, other times as a sideman. If your instrument is used alone, you should play solo performances as well.

There are four categories of musical work that you should keep in mind as you look for jobs that need your music.

Solo performers work alone. The advantage is that you are self-contained, not dependent on anyone else. The disadvantages are that all the responsibility is yours, and you have to keep yourself challenged and interested in your work. Typical soloists include pianists, guitarists, violinists, banjo players and accordionists. If you play the bass or drums, you won't work many solo jobs. The play is usually more than sideman work but less than leader jobs.

Sideman jobs are those you work as a member of someone else's group. You won't make as much money as the leader does, but neither will you have the responsibility of booking the job and keeping the client happy. Most working musicians often play jobs as sidemen, so you should get to know all the band-leaders and contractors in your area. Even established bands frequently need subs or extra players, so stay in touch. They can't call you if they don't know you.

Leader jobs are the ones you book, organise and play. When you are the leader, it's your responsibility to be sure that the job goes well and that the client is pleased. In return, the leader makes more money – often twice as much as the sideman. If you're good with people, ambitious, and well organised, you should work toward getting as many leader jobs as possible. Why work for sideman's pay when you could double your income? Of course, the leader must know how to play the job, understand what is required, and see to it that the engagement goes well.

Contractors are musicians who hire other players but do not necessarily play the job. A contractor is part musician and part agent. Typical work includes hiring musicians for large shows and travelling jobs (such as circuses and ice shows), and handling hiring for out-of-town agencies. For example, a famous entertainer doing a tour of the country may contract all the necessary musicians from one place, or may use a contractor to pick up local players in each city on the tour.

So, if you are a successful freelance musician, you should be known by those who typically contract large jobs. Also, when you begin to get calls for jobs you can't handle yourself, you can work as a contractor and arrange for other musicians to handle the engagements. Contractors are more common in large cities than in smaller, less busy areas.

Everything Must Change

Part of the difficulty in being a freelance musician today is the dynamic nature of everyday life. Not only must we keep up with changing musical styles and new equipment, but we should also stay abreast of broader changes that affect us all.

Like many developed nations, Britain is shifting from an industrial to an information-based economy, and the changes are widespread. Some cities and sections of the country will expand dynamically; others will lose population. New industries will appear, and old ones will decline. Entirely new markets for music will emerge, and the freelance player who is prepared will profit. Some examples.

- As computers become more common and personal involvement on the job decreases, the need for human contact will grow. For musicians, one outcome may be that the human interaction of the live dance band won't be displaced by the sterility of the disco -- no matter what the quality of the music. People enjoy interacting with *people* – not machines.
- Leisure time will continue to expand. Music teachers, for example, will have more students, especially for the most popular instruments (which are, in order, piano, guitar, organ, clarinet, drums, flute, trumpet).
- Electronic advances will continue to make sophisticated recording technology available on a smaller and smaller budget. Just a few years ago, good recording equipment was too expensive for small businesses, but now, cheap, high-quality studios are springing up everywhere, giving work to local writers, producers, players, singers, technicians and engineers.

You Need a System

You can succeed in music – even though there are more players than jobs – *if you know how*.

What real difference does it make to you if there are too many players? What if there are too few jobs? You don't have to succumb to statistics. All you really need to do is find enough jobs for yourself or your group. But – how do you do that?

The answer is to use a *job-finding system*. The one that's described in this book is called the *Personal Music Marketing System* (*PMMS*); I know it works, because I use it. You may devise another method that works as well for you, and if so, that's great – use it and prosper.

Realise, though, that the music business is not an easy place to make a lot of money with little effort. If you're lazy and just wait for your phone to ring, you may manage to survive – but that's about all you'll do.

On the other hand, if you use a system and apply it energetically, you'll find jobs where you didn't see them before, and you'll provide the kind of music your audience and clients need. You'll be in demand. You'll know the secrets of musical success – but they aren't really secrets. They are explained in this book. All you have to do is put them into use.

Practice makes perfect, but your Personal Music Marketing System will make money.

CHAPTER THREE

THE BASIC IDEA: MUSIC IS A PRODUCT

Music, like soap, is a product. It is produced, marketed and sold, and you should understand this process if you want to make money with your music. Those who aren't comfortable with this state of affairs will sit at home on Saturday nights and wonder why they never work.

To be successful making money from music, the musicians must also know that music is a business. This concept is as true for classical players and symphony orchestras as it is for country singers and rock bands. It applies even to religious music.

We'll call this the 'reality' of commercial music. It may not be what you'd like to believe, or what your teachers taught you, but when you try to make money by playing music, you'll have to face the facts of the marketplace.

He Who Pays the Piper Calls the Tune

The reality is that clients buy only what they need or want. Your clients will buy your music only because it will do something for them. It may entertain them, help celebrate an event, create a special mood, or simply demonstrate their affluence. But in every instance they will pay for music because it's what they need.

Rarely, or never, will you be hired just to play your own music in your own way. To be successful, you must find out what your potential clients require, and be able to fulfil that need.

Your music is a service to those who hire you, and it must satisfy them to justify its cost. Your clients usually won't be philanthropists; they aren't interested in supporting struggling artists.

To compete successfully in commercial music, then, you must follow the same strategy that every successful business-person uses;

- Develop a product – in this case, your music.
- Locate clients for your product. Do market research.
- Bring your product to the marketplace. Use sales ability to convince potential clients to buy your music.

Most musicians see themselves, rightly, as artists, and to many of them, treating music as a product seems heretical. But if you intend to make money from your music, you can't afford to feel that way.

Your music must serve a purpose for clients, or it is a waste of their money. Your job, if you make money from music, is to learn what clients need and how to fulfil their needs.

Balancing Beauty and the Business

Does this mean that to succeed in commercial music you'll have to 'sell out'? No. Successful musicians don't need to be hacks, and they certainly don't have to reject the artistry and beauty of music.

You must develop a saleable product, but this is only part of your art. Your clients buy only a little of your music for a short time. They don't own your life. Play what your clients need, if you can, but remember that your musical life is broader than any job situation.

If you plan to make money with your music, you'll have to balance the needs of your clients against your musical preferences. Most likely, you will know more about music than your clients – that's your job – but they know what they want. And they sign the cheques.

Every profession has its trade-offs, and heeding customers' preferences is one of ours. If you simply can't bring yourself to play what the job requires, then don't take it. *For some players, music is better as a hobby than as a career.*

So, does success in commercial music mean playing music that you don't like, perhaps even music of dubious quality? Yes, sometimes.

This kind of compromise is common in other professions, too . A dentist might hate doing root canals, but he or she probably does them because that's part of the job, and the dentist is in it, ultimately, for the money. An English teacher may hate teaching grammar, but if it's part of the curriculum, it goes with the position. Almost every job that pays money has some disagreeable aspects, whether it's doing root canals, teaching grammar, or playing 'In the Mood' or 'Clair de Lune' for the ten-thousandth time.

Every musician, especially freelancers who work in a variety of situations, must decide where to draw the musical line. Each player must decide how 'commercial' to be. There is no need to try constantly to play music you hate; both you and your client will be dissatisfied. Sometimes it boils down to how far you can compromise without making yourself miserable.

Professional Pleasure

There is another kind of musical pleasure you may come to enjoy – the satisfaction of 'the professional job well done.' You may find that playing only the kind of music you like is not as important to you as doing what the job at hand requires. Pleasing the client can be the ultimate measure of success.

Often there is a challenge in working out exactly what your client needs and fulfilling that need, regardless of what it is and regardless of how much you like that kind of music. A carpenter may prefer to build only modern cedar-and-glass houses, but a real sense of personal satisfaction can result from meeting the challenge of restoring an old Victorian mansion.

Similarly, you may reach the point where you enjoy – *really enjoy* – making your clients happy with your music, even when what they want isn't what you'd prefer to play. That's what it means to be a professional. When you reach that level, you're on your way to success as a freelance musician.

The Bottom Line

Music must serve a need for the consumer – or there is no need for the music. In the business of music, the quality of the work is not the central point. The central point is whether enough people will like it to be willing to pay for it.

This is equally true for the nightclub owner who hires 'personality' rather than talent and for the orchestra conductor who schedules programmes that will draw large crowds – and pay the bills.

Analyse the needs of the marketplace, fill those needs, and you'll be successful.

CHAPTER FOUR

MUSIC
IS A BUSINESS

You may be an incredible musician, but that's not enough to make you successful. To make money, you'll have to sell your music, and to do that you'll need to be business-like and organised.

Organisation is not the opposite of creativity. Organisation can give you more time to be creative. Your own music business is unlikely to succeed unless you are organised.

Being a successful musician is a lot more complicated than it might seem at first. You are a musician, of course, but you are also a part-time salesman, advertising specialist, secretary, accountant, sound engineer, equipment mover, and much more. You'll have less trouble balancing these various tasks if you stay organised, and that's not as hard as you might think.

If you rely on your memory, correspondence and contracts piled haphazardly on your desk, or important notes scribbled on bits of paper, you'll soon be in trouble. You'll forget important requirements and requests, double-book yourself, hire three drummers for the same job, or even miss engagements. This will quickly lead to a reputation for unreliability that will stop your career before it gets started.

You'll also save a lot of time – your most valuable commodity – if you stay organised. Every time you waste 15 minutes looking for a misplaced contract you have lost a quarter of an hour that could have been used productively.

Here are some ideas that will help. Keep them in mind while you work on your marketing system, and as you book more and more jobs, you'll be in control of the information that you'll need.

Getting Organised

As you develop your Personal Music Marketing System, you'll need to keep lots of information neatly at hand. Information is important in our job-finding system, and a simple filing system will supplement your memory. This does not mean scraps of paper stuffed in your pocket or filed in your wallet.

The Personal Music Marketing System discussed in this book will only work if you actually make the suggested lists and *write them down*. It won't work if you just think about it. To keep your lists and brainstorming ideas handy, you should use a notebook or loose-leaf binder. Information is essential to this system, and if you keep it in one place, you'll be able to find it when you need it. If you prefer, use the worksheets provided here, or photocopy them for use in your notebook.

A ring binder, with paper and subject dividers, is a good start. Or use a *folder* for each possible client to keep all related information together. If you don't have a filing cabinet, use a cardboard box. When you work lots of jobs, you'll never remember all the details; if you file the details you won't have to worry.

A diary is also necessary. Be sure to get one that allows plenty of room for making notes. If your kind of musical enterprise requires a lot of weekend work, be sure that Saturdays and Sundays are given the same space as weekdays in whatever diary you use. One popular type is the 'week-at-a-glance' layout that most stationers have. This will be your nerve centre, and will tell you where to go and when to be there. Don't lose it.

A pocket notebook will also be useful. One of the techniques you'll use in developing your *PMMS* will be brainstorming, and you'll get all kinds of ideas – possible clients, job leads, ideas on public-relations, songs to learn – all the time.

An expense-record book will pay for itself many times over in tax savings. Remember that you are a business-person as well as a musician, and every tax deduction and business expense that you can document will be money in your pocket.

Tickle Your Memory

You can't rely on memory alone to direct all the complicated details of your freelance music career. Will you really remember to write that follow-up letter, keep that important appointment, or post those contracts? And how will you remember to call someone who won't be back from vacation for three more weeks?

Freelance musicians, like business executives and sales representatives, have innumerable appointments to keep, tasks to perform, and important details to follow up. They need – *you need* – a systematic way of scheduling activities and making sure those activities are carried out – on time.

What's the solution? A 'memo file' to augment your diary.

Systems to jog your memory are abundant in stationery shops, but you can devise your own at less expense. Set up a folder for each month and enter chronologically the details of things to be done. Cross-reference or cue the entries to your diary.

Thus, your diary for June 6 might read, 'Letter to Acme Co.' Referring to your June memo file, you would find the notations 'June 6: sales promotion material to Acme Co. re. Christmas party. To Bill Smith Ass't Personnel Manager. Had 7-piece band last year. Budget around £700. Lots of sixties covers.' The address and other pertinent notes follow.

After you post that letter to Mr. Smith at Acme, note in your diary and memo file that three or four weeks later – say July 1 – you should follow up this letter if need be. In the memo file, be sure to mention the date of the original letter, so that you can locate it quickly for reference.

Another simple memosystem uses three-by-five-inch index cards, with monthly dividers. (If you're really busy, you could set up a card system with a card for each day of the year.) Each card contains information about one job, client, or whatever, and the cards are filed chronologically.

Whichever system you use – perhaps you'll invent your own – make it as foolproof as you can. This means that you must think of some method for ensuring that you *refer to your diary and memo file every day*. It's a great system for freeing your mind from annoying details, but it won't work unless you use it.

Knowing What's Important

Part of being organised is knowing what information is important and what's not. What should you ask? What should you save? What should you write down, and what should you try to remember?

As you sell your music to many clients, you will quickly learn that you can't rely on your memory alone. Did Mr. Jones hate rock and roll, or was it Mr. Smith? Did Champ's Restaurant want the band to start at seven o'clock or eight? Should you use the service entrance or the front door at the Seabreeze Resort? What is the client's favourite song?

This is obviously the kind of informaton you'll want to write down. Keep it in your datebook if there's enough space, or in a clearly labelled folder.

Also keep up with all the incidental information that will be part of your marketing (and musical) activities. When a client has a birthday, or mentions a favourite tune, or has a new baby, make a note to use this information for adding a personal touch to your business relationship.

If you subscribe to magazines or journals – and all musicians should – you may want to establish a cuttings file of interesting articles. A large stack of magazines is virtually useless, but an organised file of helpful articles can be a gold-mine of ideas.

Knowing Who's Important

The music business – like all others – revolves around who you know. Your network of contacts, acquaintances and friends of friends is crucial to your success. You'll need to know as many musicians, agents and possible clients as you can – not to mention secretaries and office staff. Here are a few suggestions for knowing – and remembering – who's important:

- Who's important to your musical life? Potentially, almost everybody you meet, so you should always keep your own business cards handy and be alert for possible clients wherever you go. (Business cards and other promotional strategies will be covered in Chapter 15, 'Selling.')
- Your musical career will be as much a 'people business' as a musical enterprise, so cultivate your social skills. One of the most important is the ability to remember names and faces, and this isn't as hard as it may seem. Read a book on improving your memory, and use the recommended techniques. People are flattered when you remember their names, and may be offended when you don't. Many successful club entertainers have prodigious memories for regular customers' names and favourite songs.
- To aid your memory, buy a business-card file. Ask for cards from possible clients, musicians you meet, and other contacts. Jot down pertinent information on the back of each card – such as where and when you met and what you talked about. File business cards alphabetically by name or by subject – that is, under 'agents,' 'drummers,' 'potential clients,' 'established clients' and so on.
- Establish a 'Names to Remember/Contact people' file, and keep information in it about the people you need to stay in touch with. This expanded version of

your business-card file will contain entries like 'Janice Traylor, catering mgr at Marriott's. Met 17/9/89 at Smith wedding. Needs music frequently. Has new baby. Secretary's name: Sandra Underwood.' Next time you call on Janice Traylor, you'll be able to recall these personal items and keep your relationship moving. Update this file each time you contact people; that 'new baby' will grow up fast, and secretaries move on.

Networking is a trendy American term for using personal or business contacts to further a cause or a career. Whether you call it networking or just 'being friendly,' you'll find that one good contact leads to another. People – not the best musical instruments or the ability to play a pentatonic scale at dazzling speed – are the life-blood of your profession.

One idea is to throw an occasional party – maybe on Sunday afternoon – and invite other musicians, band-leaders, agents, party planners, and as many other potential clients as you can. You'll have a chance to meet people in your field, expand your network of contacts, and maybe even make a little music. And, if you plan such a party as a business-oriented function, it's tax deductible.

The Telephone – Your Life-Line

The telephone will be your life-line. You'll use it to approach clients, book jobs, hire other musicians, and follow up after engagements. You'll spend a lot of time on the phone, so keep up with the changing technology.

Now that many customers own their own telephone equipment, all kinds of useful devices are reaching the market. You may find such items as cordless phones, automatic memory diallers, or speaker-phones to be of great value.

One thing is certain. You, as a successful freelance musician, will be spending lots of time on the telephone, so you should make it as efficient and helpful a tool as you can.

Don't forget that when used for business, telephone-equipment purchase and operating costs are tax deductible.

Answering Services and Machines

You'll probably need some kind of answering service – either human or electronic. It's pleasing to have a real person answer the phone, and answering services do. They're expensive, however, and a grouchy or forgetful operator can quickly ruin the human advantage.

Answering machines are almost universally accepted now, and most people, whether they like to or not, will leave messages. Before buying an answering machine, shop around and compare prices and features. Here are some important considerations:

- Is the machine battery or AC operated? Batteries run down, need replacing, and are more expensive in the long run. Plug-in machines are better.
- Will the machine take only 30 second messages, or is it voice-actuated to record as long as your caller talks? Voice-actuated machines won't cut the caller off in mid-sentence.
- Is there a remote beeper or other electronic method that will allow you to get your messages from another telephone? This is a very useful feature.
- Can you change the tapes yourself? Some machines rely on built-in tapes that

can't be replaced by the user. Others use simple cassettes that can be easily changed.
- When will the machine answer? Some machines will pick up only at a preselected ring – the second, for example. Others allow the user to set the machine to answer on any given ring. This is a very handy option.
- Can you vary the length of your outgoing message? Sometimes you won't have much to say; at other times you will.
- Is local repair service available? Every machine will eventually need it, and sending your unit back to the manufacturer could be inconvenient.

Consider these features before you spend your money. A few more pounds spent to get a good, well-built machine with useful features will serve you well over the years you'll use it.

Working is Taxing

You work hard to make money with your music, and you must work to keep as much of it as you can. In fact, time spent in tax planning may be more profitable to you on an hourly basis than the time you spend making the money.

Needless to say, save every receipt that could possibly document a tax deduction. Keep neat records of your music income and expenses in ink, in a permanently bound ledger. The Inland Revenue is suspicious of loose-leaf expense records.

Typical business expenses for musicians include equipment purchases and repairs, travel expenses, music and record purchases (when used for business), and magazine and professional journal subscriptions. Sales-related costs – such as printing, photography, demo tape production, and phone calls – are also deductible.

Actually, any expenses directly related to your business may be deductible, including the cost of your home office, *but these expenses must be well documented*. Consult an accountant, read up on book-keeping, and get in the habit of recording every business cost as you incur it. Even 10p phone calls add up.

Should you – a working freelance musician – really use an accountant? Yes. An accountant's services should save you more than they cost, and they may keep you out of tax trouble as well. While your tax situation may be complex to you, it will be simple to a professional tax advisor. An independent accountant can give you expert advice, calculate deductions, compile depreciation, prepare your returns, and generally help lower your tax liability.

You have to pay taxes, but you don't have to pay more than you owe. Know current tax requirements, keep your records up to date, and get professional help.

The amount of information we need to be successful increases yearly. We are living in the 'information age.' Often, what, and who, you know will be as important as what you do. The successful musician is the one who will work to stay organised and will know where to find information when it's needed.

CHAPTER FIVE

DEVELOPING YOUR PERSONAL MUSIC-MARKETING SYSTEM

Music is different from many other professions in one important way. Experienced working musicians and beginners alike face the same recurring, all-important question: how can I get more jobs? That remains the bottom line for both newcomers and established professionals. But just waiting for the telephone to ring with job offers is unnecessarily depressing.

So is just playing the same old jobs with the same group of musicians. Nothing is worse than a bad habit, and freelancers must work to stay fresh and interested. We've all seen tired, burned-out players who look too bored to hold their instruments. It's better to leave the profession than to end up this way. Fortunately, there are alternatives.

The system described in this book will help you deal positively with these problems. It offers every musician an easy, organised and personalised way to find more jobs. There's nothing complex or revolutionary about this system. In fact, it works *because* it is simple.

As music changes and your community grows, the job market will change and expand. This system will help you stay current, and staying current will help keep you interested – and interesting.

The Basic Idea The next chapters of *Profit From Your Music* explain a method that can help you systematically locate the kinds of musical jobs that will best suit your talents and interests.

If you do the brainstorming and research, if you make the lists that are the basis of the system, you will discover lots of job opportunities in your own area, and you'll have a valuable, personalised source of information that will make it easier for you to book and play engagements.

The basic idea of the marketing system is to match your own abilities with jobs that call for your kind of music. This is done in several steps.

- Assess and list your own musical skills, abilities and equipment. This will be your Personal Inventory list.
- Compile a list of every single kind of musical job that might – even remotely – need your services. Then match your skills to the jobs that require them and develop a Job Possibilities list.
- When that is well under way, you'll refine it to get a working list of Best Possibilities. This will guide your initial marketing plans.
- Expand your best possibilities list to include the names and addresses of

contact people. This will be your Good Prospects list, and these people will become your clients.

Each of these steps will be explained in detail later. You'll find it easy to create your own marketing system as you read on.

Again, it's necessary to *write down the information you compile* and really make your lists. Worksheets are provided in this book, but if you can't or don't want to write in the book, use a notebook to keep all this information together. You can't trust your memory – the system will only work if you write it down, and keeping all the lists, worksheets and brainstorming ideas in one place will save you time and effort.

Everyone Is Different

The spectrum of musical styles, types and needs is incredibly broad. It simply isn't possible to be a jack-of-all-trades musician; some specialisation is required. Rock players usually don't play classical music, and jazz musicians don't generally know country tunes.

Of course, if your abilities cover more than one category, your chances for employment are multiplied. No matter, though, how versatile you are, it's not likely that you can do everything. You'll need to target your markets to match your musical specialities.

Your PMMS will guide you in the effective use of your energy and time. It will direct you to clients who will be receptive because they need what you have to offer, and it will make your sales calls easier. Your Good Prospects list will be different from any other musician's list because it will be based on your abilities and targeted to likely clients in *your community*. It is a precise marketing tool because it is tailored by – you for you.

Brainstorming Before you can sell your music, you need to define your target clients, and you'll use several steps and methods to locate them. One of the best methods for generating new ideas in developing your PMMS is called *brainstorming*. We all sink into mental ruts or habits of thinking that limit our lives. Brainstorming frees the mind to come up with novel approaches. It's a mental exercise.

Brainstorming is a way to break down old habits and open your mind to fresh ideas and insights. It's an antidote to mental stagnation.

Here's how to brainstorm:

Find a good place to think, where you won't be interrupted – perhaps your local library, or a park bench, or even driving in the country (in which case you'd use a tape recorder instead of a notebook).

Try to put your mind in 'neutral.' Let it coast without conscious direction, and follow it wherever it goes. You'll use your memory and imagination, but you won't know where they're taking you. Don't worry. Brainstorming will lead you to new ideas.

Think about your subject – potential clients or possible playing engagements, for example – and write down every single idea that pops into your head, no matter how unlikely, foolish or absurd it might seem at first. Paper is cheap, and you are tryng to generate new ideas, so don't hold back.

Let one idea lead to another. Let your mind roam as far as possible, and let your imagination take over. Don't worry about being practical. That is exactly what brainstorming tries to overcome.

When you are brainstorming, for example, in a search for new job possibilities try to make your lists as long and full as you can. No one needs to see them except you, so don't hesitate to follow your unconscious mind as it creates ideas.

Be imaginative. Be ridiculous, but don't feel ridiculous. Be as free and open as possible. Imagine your brass ensemble playing on prime-time TV, or your fifties show entertaining on a Caribbean cruise ship. Bypass the ordinary, leap over the usual and mundane. You'll edit your lists later, but at first try to come up with new ideas. Don't try to be realistic at all. Just think freely and add to your lists!

Expand your lists through *association*. That is, let one idea lead naturally to a similar one. When your mind is coasting in neutral, ideas will automatically suggest others, link themselves together, and lead to even more new thoughts. If you've thought of playing exciting music for the introduction of next year's new car models, *association* leads you to think of doing the same thing for next year's new speedboats, computers or swimsuits. One idea leads directly – or indirectly – to another, and the more you free your mind from its habits, the more creative it will be.

Perhaps your brainstorming leads you to a client whom you hadn't thought of before, a client who will need your musical services just once a year. That's good.

If, through more brainstorming, association and research, you can find 50 once-a-year clients, you will have discovered almost a job a week. That's significant.

So don't worry if an idea seems simple, even trivial. Add it to your list anyway. Careers can be built of many simple ideas.

Always keep your pocket notebook ready for insights, names or interesting information, so that your musical employment possibilities will continue to expand. Once you start thinking in this open-minded way, you'll be constantly alert for new ideas and job possibilities. Adding to and modifying the lists that form your PMMS will be a continuing process, a never-finished project that will grow with your musical life and the changes in your community.

The More You Put Into Your PMMS . . .

The PMMS may sound like a lot of work – and it will take a good deal of time – but your preparatory work will pay off handsomely. Each client you discover and cultivate will remember you in the future, and your bank balance will grow with each job you play. Better yet, each job can lead to several others, so your list of clients and contacts will grow geometrically – until you have more work than you can handle. Thus, the work you put into developing this marketing system will be repaid in pounds, new friendships, and feelings of satisfaction for years to come.

If you really want more and more jobs, this system will get you started, and the more work you put into it, the more helpful it will be.

CHAPTER SIX

YOUR PERSONAL INVENTORY

The first list in the PMMS is a compilation of all the musical things you can do that might be saleable. Notice that I said 'might,' because you shouldn't worry about being practical at this point. If you know everything Gilbert and Sullivan wrote, put light opera on your list – even if you don't know of a single job that needs this speciality. Market research comes later. To be useful, your inventory list must be specific, and as complete as you can make it.

The Personal Inventory has three parts: a listing of your musical strengths, a listing of your equipment, and a ranking of your abilities.

Please note that this list is not only to be a compilation of the jobs you are now playing or have played. It's to be a list of what you could play now and what you might be able to play in the future. Don't be limited by your past

First, Compile Your List of Personal Musical Strengths

The first part of your personal inventory, then, is a summary of what you do best, your musical strengths. To begin, use the Personal Music Inventory Worksheet on page 22 and list everything musical that you can do. Use extra paper if you need it. *The system won't work unless you actually write this information down. You can't do it in your head.*

Don't worry yet about how good you are. Just write down everything that you have done and would like to do in music. Use your memory and your imagination.

To jog your memory and encourage you to break out of your playing habits, the worksheet is divided into several categories. They are:

Kinds of music I can play. Here, you'll list everything musical you now do at a professional, or near-pro, level. This part of your list will be the easiest to compile, since you'll list what you already know and do.

Kinds of music I'd like to play. List here the things you could do with a little work. Also list your long-term playing goals, to show where you'd like to go. If there's a style you haven't mastered, or a composer whose work you don't yet know, this is the place to list it.

Kinds of music I've played in the past. Think back to your earlier playing experiences and school days. List whatever musical activities you used to do. Did you play trumpet in the band? Were you the accompanist for the choral society? Did you play harmonica in a blues band that only performed in your garage? Don't reject anything because you haven't done it lately. Think back, and add to your list.

Kinds of music I could play – but don't enjoy. This could be the most important part of your list, because you may find that what the market needs is not exactly your favourite kind of music. Think about the commercially useful types of music that you could do, and add those categories to this part of your list. It doesn't mean that you *have* to play music you don't like, but you need a complete picture of the entire music market to make your system work.

Here's an example. Let's say that you're a freelance keyboard player. Let's assume that you have some classical piano background and that you are able to play a variety of jobs on piano, electric piano and synthesiser. We'll say that you're mostly interested in pop and rock but can play in other styles with some ease. Further, you played trumpet in the county youth orchestra and sang in college theatrical productions.

The first list in your Personal Inventory might look like this – in no particular order:

Personal Music Inventory List

Kinds of Music I can Play

Pop, contemporary
Pop, middle of the road
Rock
Disco

Kinds of Music I'd Like to Play

Jazz
Recording, jingles, demos, etc.
Shows
Teaching

Kinds of Music I've Played in the Past

Classical
Accompanying, classical instrumental
Accompanying, vocal
Church music, organ
Trumpet, in county orchestra
Vocal, in college theatrical productions

Kinds of Music I Could Play – but Don't Enjoy

Country
Solo work
Big-band work
Ragtime

Such a list would be a good starting point for a well-rounded pianist. Notice that this list only notes types of music – without ranking ability or the job prospects in each field. Some pianists can compile longer lists – more specialities, more categories.

Again, don't be concerned if your abilities are not equally developed in all par of your inventory. Every player will be much stronger in some areas than in others.

As you work on your musical inventory, remember: you don't have to be a virtuoso to make money from music. You may excel in one rather narrow field – sacred organ music, or folk guitar, for example. Don't worry, therefore, if this first list is short. You can still market your music to a select group of clients.

Don't Rank – Just List!

At this point, make no attempt to rank your talents. That will come later. Obviously, in our example, the pianist won't be as adept at classical music as at disco, or vice versa, but that's not important. What is important is defining and developing your saleable skills. You are not listing only your outstanding talents or your virtuoso abilities. You are listing everything you might want to do in music along with everything you have done or can do. Later you will concentrate on what is saleable.

To help make your inventory list as inclusive as possible, think about:

Composers. Perhaps listing the composers you're familiar with will suggest certain types of music to you.

Instruments. Thinking about all the instruments you play may suggest more possibilities for your list. If you play trumpet, does your list also include music associated with cornet, piccolo trumpet, valve trombone? If you play piano, think – for your list – about music you could perform on organ, synthesiser, harpsichord or accordion.

Use brainstorming techniques to think of musical talents that you don't normally use. Try to break out of your old thinking patterns as you compile this list.

Are You Fully Equipped?
The second part of your Personal Inventory will be a list of all the equipment you own. Use the worksheet shown on page 23. Include what's in your closet or attic as well as what you commonly use. If you are a guitarist, for example, don't forget other stringed instruments that you own – banjo, lute, mandolin, 12-string, and so on. An occasional show or recording session might call for lute, and if you can play the part, why not collect the pay? Though you may never make a living as a lutenist, an occasional job could be significant. Don't overlook any possibilities.

If you own equipment that you can't play, what should you do?

Learn to play it, if that's feasible. The more you can do, the more valuable you are. Don't spread yourself too thin, though. Don't take time away from important piano practice or from marketing your music to learn to play an old guitar you found in the attic.

Keep it, if there is some advantage in doing so. Maybe you can hire out that tuba, synthesiser or sound system even if you don't use it yourself. Or maybe your children will one day take violin lessons. Perhaps the instrument you own, but can't play, is a family heirloom or a potentially valuable antique.

PERSONAL INVENTORY WORKSHEET

Kinds of Music I Can Play _____

Kinds of Music I'd Like to Play _____

Kinds of Music I've Played in the Past _____

Kinds of Music I Could Play — but Don't Enjoy _____

EQUIPMENT INVENTORY WORKSHEET

Equipment	Model No.	Serial No.	Date Purchased	Place Purchased	Cost

Sell it. If you don't need it, get rid of it. There is no reason to store, maintain, keep up with and insure musical instruments that are of no practical use to you. You're a musician, not a junk dealer.

It is helpful to see in black and white exactly what you have; the list will help define the variety of jobs you are prepared to play.

Maybe a new piece of equipment would fill a gap or improve your performance – a new microphone, say, or a state-of-the-art synthesiser. Is there an area where you need back-up instruments or accessories? If your livelihood depends on an electric bass, shouldn't you have an extra one – just in case?

You may be astonished at the total value of your equipment once you see it listed. Be sure you have proper insurance. Expensive instruments can disappear in a flash or easily be damaged. Insurance is almost always worth its cost. Talk to several insurance agents to get a good overview of what's available.

Of course you're careful with your instruments, but you can't guard them 24 hours a day. No matter what your instrument, it can be stolen, damaged or lost. A reed player, for example, who has piccolo, flutes, clarinets, alto, tenor and baritone saxes, and perhaps an oboe or cor anglais, has a huge investment – even if the instruments are only student models. If you don't have insurance, get it.

Now Put Them in Order

Wait a few days and then read over your Personal Inventory lists. Add anything that you originally overlooked. Then loosely rank your entries using the worksheet on page 25 or your notebook. Use general categories such as 'excellent,' 'fair' and 'needs work.' Remember that if you are proficient at a style you don't particularly like, it should still be near the top of your list. And of course, if you enjoy another style that you don't really play very well, it should be ranked lower.

You may be surprised at your own musical strengths, and you'll probably find a few other areas that, with a little work, could be saleable.

Here's how the pianist in our example might rank the items from her Personal Music Inventory List. Notice that her rankings do not correspond exactly with the categories on the inventory worksheet.

Personal Ranking
1. Rock – excellent.
2. Pop, contemporarary – excellent, know all current tunes.
3. Disco – excellent, good synth technique.
4. Solo piano – good, but don't enjoy working alone.
5. Country – fair, know more standards than newer tunes. Don't particularly like this style. Easy for me to improve here.
6. Big band (thirties, forties, fifties) – pretty good but know few tunes.
7. Jazz – good, fair repertory, especially fifties, sixties and seventies standards. Weaker on contemporary tunes.
8. Ragtime/boogie-woogie – fair, don't enjoy these styles very much, know few tunes.
9. Accompanying – good with pop, fair with classical.

10. Classical – fair, poor repertoire. Rarely play, but could be 100 percent better with just a little work.
11. Church organ playing – weak because of years of neglect. Could improve quickly with practice.
12. Recording studio – little experience, but could quickly improve. Competent with many styles, good reader – should pursue this.
13. Show-playing – fair with low-pressure shows, could improve with experience.
14. Teaching – don't know, never tried, might be a good teacher. Should look into this possibility for daytime income.
15. Trumpet work – would take more practice time than I can allow. Not really commercially useful talent without lots of work.
16. Vocal work – weak, but could improve with practice and confidence. Might really improve commercial prospects if I knew tunes and sang with confidence.

Every single item on the list won't deserve your time: some styles may already be good enough, and others aren't worth the effort required to bring them up to professional quality. In this example, trumpet playing may not be a realistic market for our keyboard player, but she might decide to work on the others to bring them up to a saleable level.

Using This Information

In this example, notice the categories that our pianist has placed towards the bottom of her list – organ playing, vocal work and teaching. She could, with a little work, make these areas more commercially valuable.

PERSONAL INVENTORY RANKING WORKSHEET

Excellent _____

Fair _____

Need Work _____

Pay particular attention, then, to the bottom third of your list areas, that you don't particularly enjoy doing or haven't yet mastered. Here's where, with a bit of work, you might be able to double or triple your saleable skills.

Why? Because you've probably spent most of your time working on the kind of music you like. That's normal. Maybe the intricacies of contemporary jazz fascinate you and you spend hours perfecting stunning solos – and this skill will probably be at the top of your list. But unfortunately, there will usually be more jobs available using the skills you ranked lower. Dance work, big-band engagements, even dixieland playing will be more commercially valuable than 'pure' jazz. The marketplace isn't as musically sophisticated as you are.

This is a hard lesson to learn, but it is part of facing the reality of the music market. So look carefully at items on the lower part of your list to find untapped commercial potential.

Think Like Kelloggs

One common business practice is to survey the market to see what is needed and then develop a product to meet those needs. If Kelloggs, through market research, discovers a market for a breakfast cereal shaped like a space ship, you can bet that it will be in the supermarkets shortly.

You can apply the same idea to your music. If, later on, you find that there are lots of musical jobs in one particular area, you may decide to become proficient in that category because you know that's what the market needs – and will support.

If, then, as you complete your market lists, you discover several job possibilities in your weaker areas, it might be wise to practise a bit to bring these areas up to a saleable level. That's using the big-business approach: develop a product for an existing market.

You don't have to be in love with a style of music to make money with it. You may find that you enjoy getting paid for playing cabaret jobs, even if you don't particularly like playing that style of music.

Keep in Mind . . .

No one else needs to see your lists, so be honest – but also be creative and inclusive. Brainstorm as freely as you can. Break loose. Let your mind roam in search of fresh ideas. Your PMMS will work best if you actually write your lists down, using pencil and paper. Just thinking about it won't be effective. Whether you use the worksheets provided in this book or a separate notebook, all the information you collect will be organised and immediately available.

Again, be as complete as you can, and don't be too hard on yourself in your ability ranking. If consummate skill were required to be a success in music, many TV and pop stars would be driving trucks. Does Rod Stewart have a good voice?

Making these lists will be a continuing process, and you will add to or modify them frequently. You will find that having this information in front of you is very useful, and you'll begin to make connections and get jobs that you probably never would have otherwise considered.

Making connections between your talents and the music marketplace is exactly what the Personal Music Marketing System is supposed to do, and these lists will help guide you to new, lucrative uses for your music.

CHAPTER SEVEN

YOUR JOB POSSIBILITIES LIST

Now you have a complete assessment of your musical abilities, strengths and equipment. You know all the musical things you can do, which ones you do best, and which ones need work.

Your next task is to locate as many possible kinds of jobs as you can – jobs that will need, could use, or might possibly benefit from your music. In making this Job Possibilities list, be as creative as you can.

Again, the usefulness of the list depends on how complete it is. The more possible job categories you include, the more you'll work and the more money you will make. This Job Possibilities list will come from your experience, imagination, creative brainstorming and a little market research.

The main idea here is to think of as many different kinds or types of musical jobs as you can. Include jobs that you might be only remotely suited for. Don't worry about the practicality of opportunities at this stage. Don't even think about whether the jobs actually exist!

Especially, don't limit your list to the same old kinds of jobs you've always played. Just list the types and broad categories of musical jobs that interest you and all that you think you could possibly handle.

- Be creative.
- Engage in wishful thinking.
- Practice brainstorming.
- Spend time associating.
- Dream up some fantastic goals.

You should even try to invent jobs that would use your music. Just because no one is playing such jobs now doesn't mean you can't.

Your task here is to stay out of the ruts into which most musicians fall. There is plenty of work out there. You just have to find it, and the reward is money. It's up to you to discover that work and reap the reward.

Don't say, "I'm a guitarist, so I can only work in a rock format." Instead, stretch your idea of what a guitar can do to include other kinds of music. Can you play classical acoustic guitar? Couldn't you play solo jobs? Do you sing? How is your jazz work? Do you know standard tunes? What about playing shows? How's your reading? Have you ever taught? Are you interested in repair work?

Don't say, "I'm a vocalist so all I can do is sing in a church choir." Think instead of all the places that singing could be used, and expand your market thinking to include backing singing in clubs or at concerts, recording-studio work on jingles and demo sessions, singing at weddings, producing your own show (for conventions, trade shows, cruise ships), teaching and coaching, singing in hotels and restaurants, and playing roles in musicals. Can you sing in different styles? Do you like people? Do you enjoy the spotlight and applause? Think big. Dream creatively to expand the possible markets for your music.

When you think like this, you'll come up with other kinds of situations that could use your music. Furthermore, you might even devise jobs that neither the agents in your area nor your potential clients have thought of. Fine! You'll have that new field all to yourself.

Remember the Musical Elf

One enterprising flautist I know convinced the manager of a large department store to hire her at Christmas-time to walk around the store, dressed as an elf, playing Christmas carols. She had devised an unconventional job for herself – and a lucrative one – by thinking creatively. She had invented a job that was hers alone.

As you work on your job possibilities list, don't limit yourself to jobs that you've already played. Invent new ones! Make up a reason to have a party that will feature your music. Suggest celebrations of important – or whimsical – events.

Let your imagination work, put your mind in neutral, and brainstorm to see how many ideas you can come up with. Start with the traditional kinds of jobs that you've played, or thought of playing, and go on from there.

Now for the Mental Jogging

When you are sure that you have thought of every type of job that might possibly need you, there are still two important steps to take. First, you've got to jog your creativity again. Go back to your 'kinds of music I can do' list as a stimulant for brainstorming your newly created Job Possibilities list.

Let your mind be imaginative about each item, play association games, and see what you can come up with. Does playing chamber music in a bank lobby make you think of playing chamber music in a shopping mall? Good, you're associating, and on your way to a longer job-types list.

Second, after you've made your list as complete as possible, read the next three chapters. Don't read them now. Wait until you've expanded your own listing of job categories so that the suggestions in those chapters won't limit your thinking.

The next three chapters list many kinds of jobs for freelance musicians. Each entry includes short explanatory comments. These ideas are provided only to get you started in expanding and diversifying your own list. Your list should reflect opportunities in your own community, and it may end up being shorter or much longer than the suggestions offered here.

Remember, your Job Possibilities list will be yours alone, and the more creative you can be in discovering the kinds of jobs that can use your music, the more you'll be in demand. This list will guide you as you develop your marketing plan, so work to make it as comprehensive as you can.

CHAPTER EIGHT

KINDS OF JOBS THAT NEED YOU

Before you read the next four chapters, you should have compiled your own Job Possibilities list, and it should be as long as you can make it. I offer many suggestions here, but this isn't a 'complete' list of all freelance music job possibilities. Such a list would be impossible to compile since the freelance market is always growing and changing. These job categories cover much of the musical spectrum, and every single one won't apply to you. Some will match your situation; others will stimulate new ideas. You may be able to add entire categories not discussed here. Your final compilation should be relevant to your community needs and your own music.

Some of these jobs will fit your own abilities today. Others may be too difficult, demanding, or involved for you to play at the moment. If so, put them on your list anyway, as 'goals for the future,' and work on getting ready to play them. Some of the jobs listed here may require extensive preparation, while others may be very simple for you. Don't expect each category to be equally easy. In fact, the jobs that require the most work may turn out to be the most rewarding.

If you live in a large city or near a resort area, your list of Job Possibilities may eventually grow so long that it overwhelms you, whereas if you live in a smaller community or rural area, you will have slimmer pickings. In either case, you'll be able to find more jobs if you start with an organised and comprehensive summary of the kinds of jobs you can play.

Don't be concerned with practicality at this point. Just keep thinking of *the kinds of jobs you might possibly play.* Obviously, the more categories you list for your music, the more jobs you'll find. So keep on adding to your list and thinking up similar applications for your music.

At the risk of repeating myself, I'll say it again: *write your ideas down.* That way, you'll be building a system, not just a collection of random thoughts. As you compile your basic Job Possibilities list, however, don't be concerned about how to book any particular job. That comes later. In Chapter 12, 'Contact People,' we'll discuss how to locate the people who need your music.

Nightclubs

Nightclubs and cabarets offer an abundance of work to the freelance musician.Players who work five or six nights a week, as well as those who only play one-nighters,should keep up with the local musical scene.

There are almost as many kinds of clubs as kinds of popular music: oldies clubs, swing-music big-band clubs, country-and-western clubs, new-wave clubs, jazz spots . . . You'll find tiny bistros with barely room for a solo guitarist on a stool in the corner, clubs that specialise in huge productions of Las Vegas-style revues, and stylish restaurants that use string quartets. Whatever your speciality, you'll probably find a club that needs it.

The nightclub world is too broad to cover in detail here, but these suggestion will help you succeed.

Decide what kind of club you want to work in and concentrate on producing the appropriate style of music. Find out what type and size of band is typically hired, and act accordingly. Should four-piece groups with a female vocalist seem to be the norm in a particular type of revue, you wouldn't stand much chance with a seven-man band.

Find out what management expects before you take the job, and stay open to suggestion during the engagement. Remember, club owners are interested in filling the room and making money. As elsewhere in the music world, you'll hav to produce the kind of music your client thinks will attract customers. Don't expect to play very much original material in a Holiday Inn lounge, or a lot of ja in a Butlin's summer season.

Prepare for very hard work. Steady, every-night club engagements are physically and mentally demanding. Figure out how to stay interested in your music, take an occasional night off, and try not to succumb to boredom. Playing the same music every night for people who are mostly interested in drinking, dancing or meeting members of the opposite sex can be very frustrating.

Get a written contract. Every musician over the age of 12 has heard horror stories of crooked club owners and shady operators. If you don't get paid on Saturday, don't go to work on Monday. To gain additional clout when negotiating, join the Musician's Union.

Consider occasional work. What if you're not interested in steady, every-night club work? You should still stay in touch with club owners and the working club musicians in your area because there are other opportunities for you. A few examples:

- Often, clubs will have special events that call for extra musicians or groups – special show, or a New Year's Eve party with a large, out-of-town band.
- Some smaller clubs use music one or two nights a week only and rotate grou regularly. Weekend work might fit your schedule better than trying to play every night.
- Daytime jobs are becoming more common in some areas. Music is provided for luncheons, fashion shows, wedding receptions and business meetings tha are held in club or restaurant facilities.
- Substitute work for steadily employed musicians can offer opportunities if yo are available on short notice. When the drummer in a covers band is sick, the show must go on regardless, and you could pick up the extra work if he or sl knows of your availability.

Restaurants

Restaurants, particularly the finer, more elaborate ones, offer much work for the freelance musician. Here are some typical needs:

Background or dinner music is usually restful, soothing, sophisticated and elegant. The most frequently needed instruments are piano, accordion and guitar, but many others can be used. Flute and piano, or cello and piano, or other uncommon combinations – perhaps violin and harpsichord – provide an unusual, pleasant sound that diners will appreciate. Often, of course, typical dance bands are used.

Don't forget special holidays or particular events. Even restaurants that don't normally use music might be receptive on New Year's Eve, or on the restaurant's tenth anniversary.

Ethnic music is appropriate in many restaurants, and this can be quite exotic. If, for example, you play the balalaika, there is probably a Russian restaurant looking for you.

Many smaller cities are increasingly cosmopolitan, with mixed populations and a growing variety of restaurants – Greek, Indonesian, French, Thai, Middle Eastern, and so on. Each requires related and appropriate music.

Special events. Wedding receptions, private cocktail parties, retirement or promotion functions, and anniversary celebrations of groups or couples often take place in restaurants. A good relationship with the management can result in many referrals for parties that you would otherwise not know about.

Lunchtime music is becoming common in better restaurants and hotel lounges in some areas. Don't hesitate to suggest this idea to the restaurants in your area, particularly the ones that use music at night or have a substantial lunchtime business.

Of course, many restaurants feature the same musicians every night, but there are many occasions for extra or different music – special events, a particular week- or month-long promotion – or the need arises occasionally for substitutes for steadily employed musicians. Stay up-to-date on the restaurant world in your area.

Hotels

Because of the great number of conferences, business meetings and social events that take place in hotels, make it a priority to stay in touch with hotel people. Often they will be your best source of leads and will refer clients to you.

Moreover, hotels often have their own musical needs, including:

Music for functions. Many hotels have function or party rooms. Some larger hotels have ballrooms. All of these need live music.

Music in the lobby. Many larger hotels use soothing and sophisticated music in the lobby or lobby bar. This is particularly true during busy conventions and holiday seasons. Piano or guitar are probably most common, but this is an excellent opportunity for small pop or jazz groups, strings, or even classical players.

Music for hotel-sponsored parties. Hotels sometimes give parties for their regular clients and for their own employees.

Deputising

As mentioned already, substitute work, or 'deputising' (abbreviated to 'depping') can be an important area for freelance income. Musicians who work all those steady engagements in nightclubs, restaurants and hotels get sick, like everyone else does, and they need occasional holidays. Enterprising freelance players will stay in touch with musicians who are doing regular jobs and make known their availability.

Many musicians are justifiably afraid of losing their steady jobs; often they are only 'two weeks' notice' away from unemployment. If you are interested in doing dep work, make it clear that you are not after the job permanently and that you will not try to displace the player for whom you are depping. Other players will be more likely to hire you if they trust you.

One other thing to remember is that per-night pay on a steady engagement is usually less than you make from one-night jobs. You should be willing to dep for whatever the going nightly pay is, and the person hiring you should pay you what he or she would normally make for the time you fill in.

In large cities, deps can work frequently – perhaps as much as they'd like – simply by staying in touch with the six-night musicians in the area. The pay may be relatively low, but the work can be easy and the change stimulating.

Schools and Colleges

Schools offer a broad market for all kinds of music. Here are a few of their needs.

Peripatetic teaching for your Local Education Authority is an excellent source of income. Peripatetics, as the name implies, move around from school to school, which makes for variety. Private schools are also worth investigating; many of them employ instrumental teachers on a part-time, non-salaried basis. There are also specialist music schools, but these are few in number, and jobs are hard to come by.

Nursery schools may employ part-time music teachers to lead singing or other musical activities. If you enjoy working with children, you could become the visiting teacher at one or more nursery schools. A degree in music or education would be helpful but is usually not essential. You might even team up with puppeteers, jugglers, clowns or actors to produce simple shows for nursery and elementary school audiences.

College theatrical or musical groups will frequently need professional soloists or musicians. Watch for announcements and auditions. Often no pay is offered, but sometimes there will be a budget for adding professionals.

Accompanying for recitals, particularly near music colleges or universities with active music departments, can be a good way for pianists to make money. Pianists who are at college or university themselves can avail themselves of this opportunity if they have the time. Students are often required to give recitals, and their accompanists are usually paid.

Concerts for the student body often feature well-known entertainers or locally known groups, which frequently need backing musicians. Or if you have a packaged show that would appeal to student audiences, such as a 'History of Rock and Roll' show or an outstanding jazz revue, why not try to book your own act? Since many colleges have monthly concerts, this is a continuing market for a wide spectrum of music.

Student parties of every description have always been a staple of college life. College students love dances and parties, and for many students such events are as important as their work. End-of-year parties and balls – such as the Cambridge May Balls – provide particularly good employment opportunities. You should help students enjoy themselves with your music.

School and university reunions are held by the thousand every year. Almost all of these functions offer opportunities for music, especially music related to the graduation year.

This area has an especially appealing side for many musicians. No matter what your age – and to some extent that determines your musical priorities – there are reunions from your era that need your kind of music. If your heart is in big-band music because you went to school in the forties, you can be sure that, somewhere, the class of 1948 wants you. Or if you remember all The Beatles tunes because that's when you were in college, you'll probably find that the class of 1970 remembers those songs, too, and will enjoy reminiscing with you.

If your repertory includes songs from a particular year or era – or if you can present an after-dinner musical revue of the hits of that year – these parties could be very lucrative for you and your group.

Educational recitals in schools can be a rewarding source of daytime work. Usually the pay is not that good, but it's another string to your bow, and good public relations.

Weddings

Marriage ceremonies require many types of music, and can be a steady source of income to freelance musicians. People will get married even in bad economic times, and families usually want music for such important occasions. The use of music is not limited to wealthy families or to traditional church weddings. All marriage ceremonies can benefit from good music.

Since weddings are once-in-a-lifetime events (in theory at least), it's not unusual for families to spend more lavishly than might be expected. The music should be an essential part of the plan; remind the families involved that the entertainment cost will be only a fraction of their total expenditures.

Organists most commonly play for the ceremony itself, but almost any other pleasing instrument or combination can be used. What if you aren't an organist? People are often open to innovative ideas, so suggest different possibilities, depending on your instrument. Tell your prospective employers what you can do with harp, flute, classical guitar, woodwind quintet or string quartet. Less common instruments, such as harpsichord or lute, can be very appropriate, and the unique sound will please the bridal party and the wedding guests. Use your imagination in this category, and you'll see your job market expand.

Receptions also need music. Reception music can range from strictly background music – solo piano, harp or acoustic guitar, for example – to a large dance orchestra.

Wealthy families are often interested in bringing in an out-of-town or even a 'name' band, so cities and towns within driving distance of your home might be excellent markets.

People want their weddings to be memorable and happy occasions, and the enterprising musicians who can make practical suggestions regarding instrumentation and repertory will often be able to create more work for themselves.

Remember that although you, the musician, may be the music expert, you should become familiar with what type of music the bride and groom prefer. By anticipating and filling their musical needs, you can make yourself invaluable.

Bar Mitzvahs

Bar mitzvahs and bas mitzvahs are, like weddings, family affairs. The mood is often celebratory, and the family and guests are intent on having a good time. In some places, these events are rather rigidly styled and follow a strict pattern. In other communities, a bar mitzvah may be more like a large family party with a few horas thrown in.

The musician who is familiar with Jewish music and tradition will find a large market here, and, as with weddings, word-of-mouth advertising will lead to many unsolicited jobs. As with weddings, Jewish families will have these celebrations in good times and bad, and they offer a continuing market for freelance musicians.

Frequently there will be a reception before the dinner-dance that will call for background music, affording a good opportunity for harpists, accordionists, acoustic guitarists, pianists or small groups of almost any sort. Such occasions can be particularly lucrative to the musician who is versatile enough to play both segments – a guitarist, for example, who can play classical music during the reception and with the dance band afterwards.

Often it is up to the musician who is booking the job to think of these matters and make suggestions to the client. The father may never have thought of using harp during the reception, but if you mention it, he may love the idea. Or you might suggest a theme party to the family; perhaps an idea based on the son or daughter's interests would be appropriate. As with all potential jobs you pursue, be creative with your suggestions, and you will open many doors for your music.

You'll also find that one good job will lead to another – perhaps to several others. Word-of-mouth advertising is the best kind, and one good bar mitzvah or wedding can do more to spread your name around town than several sales calls.

Clubs

Clubs of all sorts – their variety is astounding – need lots of music for many occasions.

The most obvious clients are country and athletic clubs, with their imposing buildings and beautiful golf courses. These clubs have well-defined and regular needs for music, and should be kept aware of what you have to offer. Here are typical country club events that all freelancers should remember.

Regularly scheduled dances for club members, often on Friday and Saturday nights, sometimes use the same bands on a rotating schedule. Musicians in these bands must know the characteristics of the membership and be able to play their particular requests.

Special dances, such as on Valentine's Day or New Year's Eve, may require larger dance bands than usual. See if you or your group could be used in such a special band. There's no reason your quartet couldn't add a few pieces when a larger band is needed. Such events are planned months in advance.

Seasonal and holiday activities, sponsored by the club itself, may be as varied as the social director's (and your) imagination will allow. Your suggestions – especially if they tie in with a particular event – will be welcomed.

Athletic events, such as golf and tennis tournaments, will often begin or end with dances and parties. Keep up with each club's major athletic events by reading its newsletter. If your music is easily mobile, you might suggest a party on the tennis courts or at the eighteenth hole after a tournament.

Shows are often presented for the entertainment of club members. Sometimes a name act will bring its own support group, but often these performers will rely on local musicians. If you can play shows, be sure that the leaders and contractors in your area keep you in mind. And leaders and contractors, especially, should stay in touch with larger clubs.

Theme parties can be elaborate, and musical requirements may be quite specific. Perhaps the club's members will be involved in a fifties dance, or a roaring-twenties extravaganza, or a Hawaiian/tropical-theme party. If your speciality is ethnic, geographic or unusual music, be sure that the club's social committee knows what you can offer.

If you help the social director come up with an unusual idea to beat the boring same-old-party syndrome, you'll be an instant favourite. Always keep thinking and making suggestions.

Children's parties are another potential country club market. If you can team up with a magician, juggler, mime, puppet show or similar act, many clubs will welcome you – and pay well for your services. Again, remember that the social committee may be looking desperately for some activity to involve young people. Your suggestions can generate jobs.

Special events, which are essentially private parties given by club members for their guests, may be held in, and booked through, the club. Wedding receptions, office parties, retirement dinners, reunions, and many other such events may be held in a club's facilities. Musical needs will vary, so stay in touch.

Other clubs may not have their own facilities, but they may still be excellent markets for your music. Any group that is organised for a specific purpose may have at least one social event each year that uses music. Don't limit your job ideas to the obvious ones.

Another source for freelance music leads is the almost endless variety of organised hobby groups – philatelists, photography buffs, model railway clubs, amateur radio operators, tall-people's clubs, short people's clubs, antique car restorers, square dancers, experimental aircraft builders . . . Almost all such groups will have dances, banquets, cocktail parties, barbecues, picnics or other regular social events. They need your music.

Thus, as you compile your list, define 'clubs' as broadly as you can, but don't limit yourself just to large, established country clubs. By including every organised group you can think of, you will expand the market for your music.

Parties in Homes

Parties in homes are another special, but excellent, market. Most home parties employing musicians are given by well-to-do people. It is important, therefore, to be able to relate socially as well as musically. Perhaps an elegant dinner party will require a sophisticated piano background, or a wedding reception will need a string quartet, or a garden party will need a dance band.

Personal interaction is what these parties are about, and you should be able to talk comfortably with the hosts and guests. In fact, the better you fit in, the better you'll do at these affairs. Therefore you should take pains to look your best – and display your best party behaviour.

The non-musical aspects of these small parties are especially important. Since you are in someone else's home, you have to be careful. Don't be like the drummer who trod motor oil from his leaking van into the client's priceless Oriental rug. Don't emulate the guitarist who carelessly turned around and broke an antique vase with the neck of his guitar. Nor do you want to repeat the performance of the pianist who set off the host's burglar alarm by moving the grand piano a few inches – without realising that under-the-carpet sensors were connected to the local police station.

It's easy to scratch floors, mar walls, spill drinks, and generally make yourself unwelcome. With a little care, however, you'll avoid such pitfalls and help make the event a success. And when *you're* the one who makes the party click, you'll become a regular fixture at these soirées.

People at parties often like to stand around the piano and sing. This is good for you if you are a pianist, your repertory is extensive, and you get along well with people. The word will spread, and you will be in demand.

You may be able to 'train' the wealthy party givers in your area to expect your music at all the 'best' parties, and in doing this you may create not just a few jobs but a whole career.

If you remember names, faces and favourite tunes of your clients and their friends, they'll think you're terrific (sometimes regardless of your musical skills), and they'll want you at all their parties.

CHAPTER NINE

MORE JOBS

Public Relations and Advertising Public-relations firms and advertising agencies can be good music clients because they are involved in creating and staging all kinds of events. Whatever your musical speciality, you should let all the PR firms in your area know, so that when they have a need for your type of music, they'll know who to call.

Many of the jobs included here, and most of those in this chapter, will frequently be booked through PR or entertainment agencies. They are discussed here so you'll have a complete idea of what's involved. Whether a job is booked through an agent or directly by the musician, of course, doesn't alter what the client needs, or what the musicians are expected to perform. Here are some examples:

Political campaign appearances, fund raisers and victory celebrations are often enlivened by bands of one sort or another. Such events are often planned by the advertising or PR firm that is handling the political campaign.

New product launches can be produced with true show-business extravagance. Trumpeters with herald trumpets, for example, lend a special air to such events with colourful costumes, banners and fanfares. A car show might feature a country band for the new truck display, and a sophisticated jazz quartet for the introduction of a new line of luxury passenger cars.

Grand openings for all kinds of new buildings are often celebrated with lavish parties. Whether it's a skyscraper, multi-storey car park, or aircraft hangar, the developer's PR firm will handle the party plans, including music.

Office parties are important business functions for many professionals. Stockbrokers, lawyers, accountants and many others need a chance to socialise with current and potential clients. Their parties can be lavishly produced and often enlivened with music. Again, PR firms may hire the musicians, typically a single performer or small combo.

These events, and many more, have one thing in common: they are arranged by public-relations and advertising firms to draw attention to their client's events or products. If your music can serve such a commercial purpose, public-relations people will love you.

Public-relations firms and advertising agencies thrive on creativity and often are open to suggestions for new or unusual uses of music. When you talk to PR or advertising firms, then, be as creative as you can. Make suggestions that are too innovative to present to other clients. You will be treated as a kindred spirit.

Conferences, Conventions and Meetings

Conferences, conventions and meetings are big business. Almost every fair-sized city wants to be a convention centre, and every large hotel has a sales staff searching for organisations to hold conferences and meetings of all sorts. Virtually every business, industry, government department, social group and professional association (and there are thousands of them) has, at the least, an annual meeting or convention to discuss common interests and plan for the coming year.

This market offers an enormous opportunity to musicians; if you are aware of what the convention industry needs, you can take steps to make your musical abilities known.

Musical needs of the convention industry cover the spectrum from solo background performers to 30-piece orchestras backing the biggest names in entertainment. Convention planners often try to give their members and guests the time of their lives, and money may be no object. Music may be needed from breakfast to late night, after-hours events.

Every convention is different, of course, but here are some of the musical needs that a fairly lavish convention might have:

Breakfasts use music to wake up the troops or to set a mood, particularly if a specific theme is important to the meeting. The music is often bright and cheerful. Early-morning music may call for single performers, jazz trios, or even larger jazz combos.

If you live in an area associated with a certain type of music, then that speciality could be appropriate. Thus, male voice choirs would be big in Wales, brass bands in Yorkshire, and bagpipes in Scotland. Most convention planners like geographical specialities, whether in food or entertainment, so play this aspect of your location for as much as you can.

Daytime meetings may benefit from music for several reasons. Marches and other exciting tunes establish an upbeat tone, particularly if you are playing for a sales-oriented meeting. Walk-up music and fanfares are needed for awards.

Frequently, new products are introduced to the sales staff at conventions, and these events may be major multi-media productions in which music plays a central part. Contractors and leaders should be prepared for this kind of work.

A small strolling group can be used to announce that meetings are about to begin, and will play walk-in music for those in attendance.

Lunches need background music, of course, and again it may be related to the convention's theme. If the meeting is composed mostly of men, a female performer may be welcome, whereas a male may be preferred for a women's group. (This may appear discriminatory, but you'll often find it to be the case, and you should prepare sales presentations with this aspect of the business in mind.)

Because those attending usually talk business during lunch, subdued music is often desired. Luncheons offer a good opportunity for the unusual instrument or group, so music that is not appropriate for dancing will often be chosen for lunchtime music.

Special events may be held for the families of those attending large conventions, and they'll present musical opportunities. Convention planners often wonder what to do with, and for, the spouses and children of convention-goers. If you make specific suggestions involving your musical talents, you may increase your bank balance considerably.

Cocktail parties and hospitality suites are mainstays of the convention industry. Often, the real business of the convention – the wheeling and dealing – will take place in the informal atmosphere of a hospitality suite. Frequently, your client will not be the convention itself, but a related business or association.

Thus, at a bankers' convention there might be several hospitality suites sponsored by large banks and the companies that serve them – perhaps computer firms, software providers, office-furnishings dealers, and large printing outfits. Many of these companies will spend enormous amounts of money to please and impress their clients, and the freelance musician can often be an important part of the hospitality suite's success.

Musical needs of hospitality suites can cover the musical spectrum. Often a single piano, accordion, violin or guitar may be appropriate, but just as frequently, a small combo that can start the evening with background music and gradually shift to dance music will be wanted.

Sometimes, a particular kind of music will be suggested by the season – Christmas songs in December, for example.

The hosts, in cocktail party or hospitality settings, are anxious to impress their clients, and musicians can help by making creative suggestions. If you can consistently provide the kind of music that's needed, you can become an invaluable resource to the conference organisers in your area.

Whatever your musical speciality, there is probably a need for it somewhere in a convention hospitality suite!

Convention dinners can be elaborate, and will often need background or dance music. The music may be linked to the convention's theme. Perhaps the band will need to play national anthems or state songs to salute those in attendance. Perhaps a baroque ensemble will be needed, or a barbershop quartet to serenade the attendees. Maybe the organisers would like country music, or a performance by the local symphony orchestra, or a jazz band. Anything goes.

Dances are held in conjunction with many conventions. They offer to those attending a chance to relax and socialise – and talk a little business at the same time. Two basic factors influence the kind of music that will be required.

First, the convention-goers will want to talk. That's why they're together in the first place. So the music can't be too loud. Second, the crowd will probably be quite mixed in ages and backgrounds, so a variety of music will be needed.

Whatever your speciality – whether it's fifties rock and roll, forties swing music, or old-fashioned music hall songs – be sure to let the party planners know so that your music can be a central part of their events.

Convention work covers a broad spectrum, and includes virtually any kind of music. The organisers who put these meetings together, and the booking agents who work with them, are looking for entertainment – sometimes desperately. If your suggestions, backed by a good reputation and professional appearance, can help them avoid the 'same old thing,' you'll be appreciated and in demand.

Sales Conferences

Sales conferences are similar to conventions, but are usually smaller and are produced by individual companies. Music is sometimes used to motivate employees and excite others in the audience about the company's plans and products.

In sales meeting situations, you need to realise that music, while important, plays a secondary role. The upbeat atmosphere is what is crucial, and there may be little or no room for musical subtlety. If you don't like the sound of this, sales meetings may not be for you. On the other hand, these events aren't too demanding, and they offer daytime income, a plus for most freelance musicians.

A company may be giving away a trip as a sales incentive, and in such a case the music will be thematically related to an exotic destination – maybe Hawaii, Spain or the Bahamas. Get this information in advance, and be prepared with the appropriate instrumentation and repertory – maybe even specially hired costumes.

Businesses

Businesses of all kinds are good possibilities for a great variety of music. Large companies, department stores or professional firms will be good prospects, but don't overlook smaller concerns.

Each business-related musical need may apply to dozens – or hundreds – of different companies. It's up to you to relate your ideas and your kind of music to department stores, insurance agencies, car dealers, manufacturing plants, and so on. Tracking down all the musical opportunities in the business world could be a full-time job.

Often, these events will be produced by advertising, public-relations or entertainment agencies. Larger companies in particular will leave the details to such outside party planners, as discussed at the beginning of this chapter, and you'll need to stay in touch with the agencies in your area to book these jobs. Other companies, however, prefer to plan and put on such functions themselves, so don't overlook the possibility of booking these jobs directly when you make your marketing plans.

Here are several types of business event that may need your musical services:

Grand openings of anything from factories to department stores can be celebrated with upbeat, inspiring, exciting music.

Seasonal sales could feature anything appropriate – for example, a brass band at a car dealer's for September's introductory sales, or an elegant flute and harpsichord duo in a fashion boutique for the new season's styles. Your creative suggestions in this area could get you the job.

Trade shows, where business-people meet to sell products and swap ideas, frequently use different kinds of music. Trade shows are like conventions, but concentrate on displays and products instead of meetings. Your job may be to attract people to a particular booth or display. New-product launches, particularly, need exciting music.

Promotions and retirements are often celebrated with elaborate parties. Even the more formal firms will relax a bit on these occasions and use background or dance music – maybe even in the office. Retirement parties, obviously, should feature the guest of honour's favourite songs.

Company milestones such as anniversaries, corporate acquisitions, or new construction need to be celebrated and will often need music of some kind.

Christmas parties offer many opportunities. Almost every company has at least one Christmas party. Large concerns may have several: one for the executives, another for the professional staff, and a third for the lower-level employees. Start planning early for the busy December season.

Fashion shows are given by department stores, boutiques, merchandise marts, trade associations, clubs and other groups. They may be held in hotel ballrooms, clubs, theatres, restaurants or schools. Music is a crucial element, yet sponsors often rely on taped music that is inflexible and frequently of very poor quality. You should sell the show organisers on using you or your group because of the added flexibility and the excitement of live music.

Musical requirements will vary according to the nature of the audience, the clothes being shown, and the desires of the director. Some fashion shows will be composed of little more than a few models wearing new clothes and walking through the lunchtime crowd at a fashionable restaurant. Others will be elaborate productions, carefully scripted and planned, and bordering on the complexity of a stage show. Such events will require rehearsal and careful coordination of the music with the clothes being shown; the musician's job is to create a stimulating and appropriate atmosphere.

Part of your task at a fashion show may be that of a translator. You will be asked to provide music to match the clothes or to create a certain mood, and you will probably have to translate such terms as 'sophisticated,' 'bouncy,' 'urbane,' 'chic' or even 'new' into music. It will help if your repertoire is broad and you don't have to rely on reading all the music you play. Speed and flexibility are important.

Associations

In today's information-based business and professional world, people with similar interests are increasingly joining together in associations to share knowledge and data – and to socialise. Many people get an important sense of belonging from membership in an association, and sometimes it's hard to separate the social aspects of associations from their professional and business purposes.

Associations represent everybody from red-headed people to makers of liquid fertiliser, from doctors of neurology to Trivial Pursuit players, and from Renaissance music fanatics to college teachers. You will be encouraged upon learning how many of these groups are active in your community (the Yellow Pages will get you started in your search) and how many of them use music at their functions.

Associations hold regional and national meetings or conventions. You should certainly become aware of the enormous number and variety of associations that are active in your area, because many of them will have dinners, fund-raising events and dances that need music, not to mention those annual conventions.

Large associations often book large dance bands or even complete after-dinner shows, while smaller groups use combos or single musicians. Perhaps the members will have a talent show or other activity that you could play for, or perhaps they'd like to feature *you* as the evening's entertainment.

Civic, Social and Non-Profit Organisations

After-dinner shows, dances and fund-raising events are frequently put on by civic associations and social organisations, and they need music. Some have their own facilities, with regularly scheduled dances and social functions. Others will have infrequent social events. The freelance musician should stay in touch with all such organisations and be aware of their changing musical needs.

Often, the social or entertainment committee changes each year, and the new officers may have no idea of who to call to book a band or after-dinner show. They will appreciate learning what you have to offer.

Fund-raising events can be elaborate. Some organisations may put on extravagant shows requiring many rehearsals, elaborate costumes, and so on – all to raise money for the group's projects.

Since the fund-raising market is a large one, the musician should be aware of all nearby non-profit organisations. Don't forget historical preservation societies, opera companies, theatres, health organisations, specific disease-related foundations, and even athletic associations – all of which may sponsor dinners, dances or shows to benefit a cause.

Parades, fairs, carnivals, street parties and many other events are also used to raise money or get publicity. Know which civic association sponsors them.

You may be asked to donate your services, and if you do you may be able to take a tax deduction for the value of your contribution. But many fund-raising organisations will pay for your musical services, just as they pay for the food they serve, and raise the money from the public. A few benefit gigs may be helpful as advertising, but many might be financially counter-productive.

Government-Sponsored Work

You pay rates and taxes, so why not try to get some of that money back by working for local or national government? Although governments aren't usually thought of as buyers of music, you may be surprised at the variety of jobs you can find through the bureaucracy. Here are a few examples:

Municipal parks offer ideal locations for outdoor music-making during the summer months.

Inner-city festivals, grand openings of newly renovated areas, and parties to celebrate special days are commonly produced by local Councils. When it's an important anniversary in the history of your town, why not suggest a concert in the park or a street party? The Council may conduct the affair directly or work with a private-sector sponsor.

Cultural projects, particularly ethnic ones, are widespread, and government-sponsored music at National Trust and historic sites offers interesting opportunities.

Foreign tours to entertain our troops overseas provide work for musicians, entertainers and groups. Many musicians have spent enjoyable (though hardworking) summers doing tours of European and other military bases.

Each branch of the armed forces has its own bands, and these offer secure employment, travel and excellent musical experiences for musicians who are interested in full-time playing jobs. Many of these bands are of an extremely high standard. Often, too, armed-forces band members can accept outside freelance work to augment their incomes.

Officers' clubs and NCO clubs on most military bases need bands for regularly scheduled dances and for special occasions. Sometimes, units from the base's band supply music, but usually outside groups are hired. If you live near a large military establishment, it could provide you with a substantial amount of work.

Grants, scholarships, stipends and student loans are offered by government as well as by private foundations or organisations. Each grant or scholarship will have specific requirements and be for a specific purpose, but if you have a musically worthwhile project that needs funding, you should research such sources of money.

CHAPTER TEN

STILL
MORE JOBS

Theatres and Shows

Theatres, both amateur and professional, need music. Musicals must have accompaniment, from rehearsal pianists to pit orchestras. If you are an instrumentalist and a good reader, then playing shows as they come through your area may provide a considerable portion of your freelance income.

If you are a singer, you should be aware of the chorus or backing vocal needs of all the shows that come to town. This includes theatrical productions, concerts and nightclub acts.

In many places, several theatre companies aspire to professional status but constantly battle to survive. These semi-professional theatres may not offer much money, but there should be some compensation. This is an excellent way to get experience and meet people in your field.

Shows featuring famous entertainers pick up local musicians for the orchestra. Well-known acts will often travel with a conductor and pianist and hire all other players locally. Since the theatre season can last several months, this can be an especially lucrative market for those players who enjoy it.

Your own show. If you are an entertainer as well as a musician, you may want to produce a show and book it to civic groups, conventions, fairs, festivals and even cruise ships. To be effective, a show must be well conceived, well written, professionally produced, and – above all – entertaining. Elaborate and expensive productions on television have set the standard for today's audiences. If your singing, jokes, choreography, costumes and – most important – charisma and stage presence don't measure up, you'll find it difficult to succeed.

Since audiences expect a high level of entertainment, you'll have to work hard to put together a successful show. If you do, however, you'll have a very saleable product that can be booked 'as is' for years. Many successful performers – singers, comics, instrumentalists – develop a format that works well and rarely change it.

The market for shows is huge and expanding. Once you've created a successful show, however, your work isn't over. You have to maintain your product. What happens if the featured vocalist gets pregnant? Or goes back to college? Or your guitarist wants to produce his own show? No one ever said that show business would be easy, but if entertaining is in your blood, give it a try.

Entertainment, fast-paced and energetic, is what show business is all about. Few instrumentalists can carry an entire show; usually a singer or vocal group is the main attraction. Some solo acts, of course, are very popular and well known to the general public, but dozens of lesser-known groups travel the country with considerable success, even though they may not be widely acclaimed.

Circuses and Travelling Shows

Circus playing is similar to playing shows, but it is much harder work and happens only once or twice a year. Brass players particularly should stay in touch with local contractors and band-leaders to be in line for this work.

Other road shows – ice shows, and so on – will use local musicians These shows will visit all medium-sized and large cities and can provide a week of well-paying work for those who are able to read the charts – and endure the physical demands of non-stop playing.

Tourist-Related Jobs

Tourist-related work may be plentiful and lucrative in your area, but you may need to use your imagination to find – or create – it.

Historical sites suggest many musical applications. Start by investigating National Trust sites in your area. You might double your chances if you also make, for example, lutes or recorders. By combining this craft with the appropriate music, you could make yourself a featured part of the tourist attraction.

Sightseeing tours sponsored by local companies for convention-goers or other touring groups may need special music at various destinations or even on the tour bus, boat or train itself.

Cruise ships take thousands of tourists yearly on elaborate holiday jaunts, and use dance bands, show groups and single performers to provide entertainment for their guests. Headline acts may be well-known performers, but there are numerous opportunities for versatile backing musicians. Sometimes, there are special cruises for classical music lovers, featuring chamber music, small orchestras and famous soloists.

A restored theatre in your area may provide another opportunity. Visiting groups would enjoy a short show featuring music of the building's original era.

Seasonal festivals or neighbourhood celebrations attract many visitors and need a variety of music. Why couldn't your chamber music group work with the botanical gardens activities committee to coordinate a concert in the gardens? Or a recital in a restored mansion during the candlelight tour of homes?

A famous composer or performer from your community need not be alive to help you. A programme of his or her music might be just the thing to perform at the birthplace or memorial centre – or as an after-dinner show for civic or convention groups.

The possibilities for tourist-related music are almost endless. If you match your imagination and musical ability with some creative marketing, you may find jobs where none had existed before.

Orchestras

Orchestras frequently use supplementary musicians for special concerts, adding extras as the music demands. Good freelance players with appropriate backgrounds should be alert to this possible source of employment.

Classical freelance players can often get work with amateur, student or even professional orchestras. Often, amateur and student symphony orchestras or chamber groups will bring in section-leaders and soloists from outside for concerts, so expand your job-search to include such musical groups.

Classical players in London often play with smaller symphony orchestras in cities within a 200-mile radius – Cambridge, Bristol, Reading, and so on. The market for their music is thus expanded from one to several cities.

Every large city helps support the arts in smaller surrounding communities in this way, and the willingness to make a few hours' drive can improve your market outlook.

Churches and Synagogues

Churches and synagogues offer several employment opportunities to a wide variety of musicians. Here are a few possibilities:

Church choirs – especially the larger ones in large cities – may pay their soloists or even their members for performing at regular weekly services. Frequently, freelance help is used for special festivals or concerts.

Weddings and funerals need music. Sometimes music for these occasions is taken care of by staff musicians, but often, outside freelancers are hired. Remember, too, that traditional weddings can involve much more than organ and piano, and that contemporary services can use virtually any kind of music that appeals to the bride and groom.

Stand-in organists, pianists and choral directors may be needed by churches or synagogues on short notice. Religious services must go on even when the regular organist or choir director is sick or on holiday. If you are available and competent to do fill-in work, let it be known.

Holiday programmes often provide a yearly busy season for both vocalists and instrumentalists. One freelance bassist I know regularly plays five or six performances of *The Messiah* during the Christmas season – all paid, of course, and all with paid rehearsals.

The freelance player must be aware of these opportunities and be prepared to do an excellent job with little rehearsal. Even churches that have access to good amateur musicians who play for free sometimes hire professionals to do a better job and save rehearsal time.

Staff positions are not really in the freelance category except perhaps as part-time work; they do offer employment opportunities for the trained organist, pianist and choir director.

Rehearsal pianists, especially in larger churches, are needed for extensive choir programmes. The pay may be unexciting, but the work should be pleasant and regular.

Novelty

Novel uses of music are the products of imagination and are perfect examples of the creative approach. The following ideas are for you to consider for your list of possibilities and for stimulating your own imagination. In one way, novel jobs are like all others in the freelance music business: they are where you find them – or make them.

The 'singing (or playing) telegram' is one new, and growing, market. If you are outgoing and funny, are blessed with creative flair, and have, perhaps, a touch of the bizarre, you could do well here.

Street musicians working in many large cities make an art of making their own jobs. This kind of music offers direct communication between player and audience. If they like your music, you make money. If they don't, you starve.

If you are adventurous and something of a showman, you might consider this form of contemporary minstrelsy.

Don't be limited to the same old traditional jobs. With novelties in music, you can be as creative as possible. Think of a job to match your talents, and then sell or try out the idea. A trumpet player I know has played more than one wedding fanfare from a hot air balloon hovering over the site of a ceremony.

Music-Related Jobs

Don't overlook non-performing, but music-related, jobs: you can often profit from your expertise in non-playing ways. Some of these could even lead to a career or new professional directions for you. Here are a few suggestions; you'll think of others that may better match your talents and interests.

Radio and TV jobs requiring musical knowledge include programme planning and on-the-air work. If you're a true jazz buff, for example, you might produce a weekly jazz show for a local station – or a country, folk or chamber-music hour if that's your speciality. Perhaps you could use your expertise in the programming field, or even in selling broadcast advertising time.

Music libraries are specialised departments requiring trained librarians. A qualification in librarianship combined with your musical knowledge, could start a new career.

Music therapy also requires special training, but qualification combined with your performing background might lead to a satisfying career helping people through music.

Music criticism may be satisfying for musicians who also like to write. Local newspapers, magazines and broadcasting stations all need music critics. If you understand music, the qualities of a good performance, and the essentials of writing clearly, part-time music criticism may get you free tickets, free records (if you write record reviews), *and* a pay-cheque.

Private Teaching

Once you become proficient with your music, why not share your knowledge and skill with others? Teaching music offers a stable way to augment your income, and could become your main occupation. But teaching isn't easy. It requires patience, organisation and the ability to demonstrate and explain difficult concepts.

For some kinds of music teaching, in-depth training is required, but for other musical styles, professional experience is more important. If you want to teach at an advanced level, for instance, classical piano – you'll most likely need a music-college qualification. If, however, you want to teach improvisation – a skill not always taught in college – you'll need to be an excellent jazz/pop player yourself.

One pianist I know is more interested in jazz and his own compositions than in pleasing commercial clients. He finds that teaching jazz and improvisation offers him a sizeable income without the pressures of performing music he doesn't enjoy. He has 50 students and gets £15 per hour lesson. Because he enjoys teaching, he doesn't mind working in the same studio all day.

To prepare yourself for teaching, you'll need to organise your approach, determine what you have to offer, and attract students. Often, you can work with school music teachers and music shops to find pupils. Word-of-mouth advertising is the best kind. One satisfied student will quickly lead to another.

How much can you make? How much should you charge? Teaching fees vary widely – depending on where you are, how much education and experience you have, what you teach, and how much competition you have – but most musicians can add significantly to their income by taking at least a few students. Find out what other teachers offer and charge, and price your services accordingly. Read books and magazine articles on music teaching to get more ideas on this important aspect of professional music.

Technical Assistance

Technical assistance is increasingly significant to musicians because electronics, sound reinforcement and computers are now an important part of the music world.

Only a few years ago, for example, a pianist was just that – a pianist. He or she would simply walk in, sit down at the house piano, and play. Today, even the name has changed. The term is now likely to be 'keyboard player' or even 'synthesist,' and familiarity with electronics, synthesised sound and computers may be as important to the performance as musical ability.

Musicians who are technically inclined and trained and who understand these newer aspects of the business may find many jobs waiting for them.

Younger or less experienced players might find 'roadie' work a good way to gain experience. Carting electronic pianos, guitars and drums, or setting up and running sound equipment should not be left to non-musicians.

Sound reinforcement is an increasingly important area of contemporary music. The way a group sounds can depend more on the sound engineer than on the players themselves. This is true for classical ensembles as well as rock performers. Even novice local bands often depend on a sound specialist to keep the sound 'right' out front.

Teaching electronic music techniques is a new opportunity for those who understand changing technologies. Synthesists, for example, may find work teaching other keyboard players how to programme their new instruments. Since many pianists are confused and frightened by the new wave of electronics, enterprising synthesists will probably find many students if they can share their knowledge.

Synthesiser programmers can also find work in recording studios or at special promotions in music shops and at trade shows. Some synthesiser masters create and sell programmes on cassette tape – ready to be loaded into the memory of popular synthesisers – and they advertise this service in music magazines. This is a perfect example of enterprising musicians taking advantage of changing technology.

Repair Services Instrument repair is another promising area for technically minded musicians.

The traditional fields of instrument repair and piano tuning are excellent sources of steady work for qualified technicians, and the repair field is expanding because of the new, complex electronic equipment now being widely used. The musician who can repair amplifiers, electronic keyboards and related equipment will be in demand.

Instrument and equipment repair is not, of course, a strictly musical skill, and many repair people are not musicians at all. However, musicians who are competent at repair work will have a distinct advantage, since they will be able to communicate directly with their customers and understand exactly what is needed.

Musicians who are interested in electronics and technology may find that technical colleges in their areas offer low-cost or free training in electronics. This training and subsequent work won't interfere with night music jobs, and can open new career doors for technically adept musicians.

Sales You know you'll have to sell your own music to make money from it. That's what this book is all about. But selling yourself and your music is not the only profitable way to combine music with selling. Becoming a music salesman, part-time or full, is another.

If you enjoy working with people, you might enjoy sales, as well. So consider:

- Selling in a music shop. Many of today's instruments are so complex that knowledgeable sales-people are in demand. If you understand synthesisers, for example, why not get a job demonstrating and selling them? You'll acquire steady daytime income, stay up-to-date on new developments, and get a discount on your own purchases.
- Selling in record and sheet-music shops offers the same advantages. Your specialised knowledge of the field will make you especially valuable to the shop manager, and you'll get a chance to increase your involvement with music.

An extra benefit is that a music shop is often a centre for a community's musical activity, so you'll keep up with what's going on with bands, musicians and jobs in your area.

Most music shops are locally owned, and you can deal directly with the owner or manager. You may also find selling jobs through employment agencies or classified ads. Describe your musical background, but concentrate on your selling abilities – even if they're unproven. Music-shop owners, like nightclub managers, are more interested in profits than in musical ability.

Never sold anything? Don't think you could? Don't worry. If you're interested in this field you can develop selling skills. There are many excellent books on sales techniques.

Writing, Arranging and Copying

Writing, arranging and copying can be a lucrative side-line for many freelance musicians. Depending on your talent and skill, there are several kinds of writing that you may do:

Writing lead sheets for soloists, vocalists, bands or shows is a much-needed talent. (Lead sheets are transcriptions of individual songs, with only the melody line and supporting chords indicated – a bare minimum that leaves interpretation up to the performer.) This may involve simply transcribing melodies and chords from records. Or it may require working with composers who don't read music. Singers, particularly, need lead sheets in their keys, and this is an area where a bit of expertise will be lucrative. Since there is a steady supply of new bands and vocalists who need lead sheets of current tunes, this market can provide a dependable part of your income.

Writing full arrangements and scores is a much more challenging field, and usually requires special training and study. Good arranging skills are rare, and a freelancer who is a gifted composer/arranger may have as much work as he or she can handle. Typical jobs include creating special arrangements or scores for audiovisual productions and films, and composing advertising jingles.

It is not uncommon for a player who writes a little to evolve into a writer who plays a little. Good writers and arrangers in such a specialised field as advertising-jingle writing may make much more money than the players who record their music.

Copying the music that others write requires a meticulous mind and close attention to detail. Good copyists, particularly in large cities, can make substantial incomes, though synthesiser-computer-printer technology may eventually have a substantial impact in this field.

If you enjoy calligraphy, are creative with pen and ink, and know music well, you might augment your income through copying. Certainly, every musician who plays a clear, well-written chart will thank you.

Songwriting is not – at least for the beginner – a dependable way to make money. It does offer the chance to write hit songs and collect royalties for a long time. That possibility, however, is fairly remote because of the enormous number of people diligently writing and submitting songs. Don't quit your job to become a songwriter, but if you like to compose music or write lyrics, be persistent. It's hard to get started, but once your name is known, you'll be able to get your work heard.

Recording

To many people, *recording* means record albums, hit songs, the quest for gold or platinum records, and the fast-lane world of the pop celebrity. The record industry is, to be sure, a large and very visible part of the music world, but recording fortunately can mean much more than striving for hit records.

The desire to make a big record is natural, but the chances for success are remote. According to some estimates, a *fantastic talent* with a *fantastic demo* has about a 6,000 to 1 chance of getting an album deal, which is merely the beginning of the road to recording success. Pursuing this avenue requires a heavy investment; the necessary video may cost £10,000 for a bargain-basement production, and a decent album itself could be another £50,000 to £75,000. Worse yet, these expenses are not paid by the record company.

But as depressing as the odds against recording a hit record may be, there is plenty of other work in the recording industry for all kinds of musicians. Since this market is expanding, all musicians should think of recording as a potential market. Demos, jingles, audiovisual and film scores, video production, multi-media concert events – all are growing markets for recorded music.

This is an area where changing technology is having a rapid impact. Advanced, compact and less expensive recording equipment has recently made it possible for smaller studios to have excellent recording facilities. More recording studios mean more work for musicians everywhere. No longer is recording the exclusive domain of a few expensive 24- and 48-tracks.

There are several different kinds of recording sessions.

Jingles are musical commercials for businesses, and sometimes for non-profit organisations, and government campaigns. The money, time and energy spent on a 30- or 60-second commercial may be unreal in every sense, but the musician's job is to do just what is asked. Never mind that the extremely difficult part you play may be inaudible in the final mix when the voice-over is complete!

On the other hand, you may help produce an award-winning and popular jingle that becomes part of the consciousness of everyone who watches TV or listens to the radio.

Payment for playing in jingle sessions ranges from fairly low for local, limited-use spots to extravagant for union players and singers who receive residuals for long-running fully networked commercials.

You may find that the recording musicians in your area form an informal clique, and it may be difficult to get started in this potentially lucrative area. If you aspire to this kind of work, however, it will be worth your while to keep trying to become a regular player on jingle sessions.

Demo sessions produce demonstration tapes of some sort – perhaps for a songwriter, a singer or a band. Since these tapes are usually financed by one person (a songwriter, for example) rather than a company, the pay may be quite low. Demo sessions, however, provide a lot of work for studios and musicians, and can lead to more important, higher-paying studio jobs.

Almost every small town now has at least an eight-track studio and often will support several large enterprises. The commercial recording market will continue to grow, and will rely increasingly on freelance musicians to provide music for a variety of needs.

Record sessions for major labels can be very rewarding, and top-flight studio players are among the most competent, accomplished and best-paid musicians anywhere. Consequently, this area is among the most difficult markets for most players to enter. But even if you never play a session for one of the majors, there's plenty of work on the next rung down for the smaller independents. The pay won't be as good, but you can still make a decent living.

Miscellaneous recording work includes production of audiovisual and film scores, recordings for sales meetings, and music for television shows. A large company, for example, may want upbeat, exciting music to enliven its awards presentations. Rather than depend on hiring a live band, the company decides to use recorded music. Or a comedian may want to record backing music because his budget won't always support a live band. Such recording sessions are typical of a small studio's work, and the variety can be as stimulating as if a platinum album were the goal.

All freelance players who are capable musicians and good readers – and who understand different styles – should stay in touch with nearby studios. There may be few calls for a bassoonist, but when a bassoon is needed, nothing else will do.

Recording work is an excellent goal for all musicians, and it can be exciting and well-paying. In many cases, however, only the best, most versatile, and most persistent musicians will be able to find work regularly in demanding studio settings. Highly developed playing skills are often required.

You must have so mastered your instrument that you can play whatever is set before you – and play it well. Most recording sessions allow little rehearsal time – maybe once or twice through the part – so excellent sight-reading is essential. Music on tape is unforgiving. Intonation problems, rhythmic inaccuracies, or other lacks of precision will be painfully obvious. Nothing is as embarrassing as making the mistake that requires another 'take,' causing more work for everyone and costing the client more money in studio time.

In some recording sessions, 'head charts' are used. These are very rough sketches instead of completed arrangements. There may be no written music at all. In such sessions, your ability to improvise is critical. You should also be adept in many styles. The producer may ask the pianist, for example, to try a Donald Fagan-style sound – or Billy Preston, or Erroll Garner, or virtually anyone. In these situations, the pianist would be expected to know – and be able to provide – whatever style the producer wants. Sometimes you may even make 'record copies,' particularly for commercials where the ad agency wants to create the 'sound' of an old record without using the record itself.

Because studios normally charge by the hour, mistakes caused by becoming rattled under pressure can be expensive and incur the wrath of the producer or the client. Nervousness in the recording studio is taboo. Instead, you need to be relaxed and self-assured.

Booking

What if you get several calls for a band on a busy Saturday night? Should you simply tell the callers that you're already working? Why not do a little booking yourself?

If you're well organised, know enough musicians, and attend properly to details, you can add 'part-time booking agent' to your list of freelance opportunities. To book a group occasionally, you'll line up the musicians, send the contracts, double-check with the client and the band-leader, and collect a commission. On a smaller scale, you could agree on a finder's fee or referral charge with other musicians, say, £20 for each job you refer.

Probably the most useful attribute a booking agent can have is the ability to sell, to talk easily with people, to persuade. In this area of the music business, selling ability is much more important than playing talent. If you are outgoing and like selling, you may do very well as an agent.

Should you want to start a full-time booking agency, you'll soon realise that it's nearly mandatory to have prior experience in this competitive field. Try, therefore, to work for an established business before striking out on your own. As with any business, you'll have to deal with book-keeping, taxes and other details. Booking as a full-time job may look easy, but it isn't.

Hard work or not, you can make quite a bit of money in this area of the business. If you book all the entertainment for a convention with a £30,000 entertainment budget, your commission should be several thousand pounds. Furthermore, if you regularly book players for weddings, receptions or other events, you could easily make an extra hundred pounds or more weekly.

If you're just starting, try to get a job – clerical, secretarial or sales – with an established agency to learn how the business operates. For a fully-fledged booking business, an extensive network of contacts, both in music and in every part of the business community, is essential to generate a substantial amount of work.

Now Take Time Out to Look Over Your List

You should now have many entries on your list of jobs possibilities, and your own compilation is probably quite different from this one. Yours might be longer, or shorter, and it might include jobs that aren't discussed here at all.

Now is not the time to be exactly critical of your list. It is the time, however, to review your list to see if you have followed the guidelines stated earlier. Here are a few questions to keep in mind as you look back over your ideas for jobs that need your music:

- Have you written down every job idea you yourself might possibly handle – no matter how apparently outlandish or far-fetched – or even silly – it seems?
- Have you brainstormed for new uses for your music, or have you restricted yourself to ideas listed in this book?
- Have you practised your association techniques to expand your list to include similar, but new uses for your music?
- Are the entries relevant to your own instrument(s), musical tastes and ability?
- Have you limited your list to the kinds of jobs you have already played or have you branched out, expanded your horizons?

Opportunities in music go far beyond playing in clubs, in churches, or at concerts. As you work on your Job Possibilities list, add non-playing, but music-related, items like those mentioned or ones you dream up. The idea, once again, is to create as broad a market list as you possibly can. Maybe your interests will direct you towards music therapy or broadcasting, for example. Perhaps you will have to get a degree to achieve your ultimate ambition. But you'll be working with music and working toward a goal. It's hard to beat that combination.

The Job Possibilities list you have made and are about to look over is yours and yours alone. You are going to use it later as a worksheet for planning exactly how to market your musical wares. The list you finally end up with will be the one you use to find work, create jobs, and earn more money for yourself. Better that your list is too long than too short, for the idea you discard today might appeal to you tomorrow.

While you look through your list – mostly to see what you've omitted – let your mind roam. See if you can invent a new use for your music – create a need as the advertisers sometimes do – and highlight it on your ever-expanding list of possible jobs.

CHAPTER ELEVEN

YOUR BEST POSSIBILITIES

Now you should have a long list of possible jobs that could use your music. You have really tried to go beyond the same old routine engagements that you've always played, because creativity and flexibility are necessary to keep up with the changes in your community. You also know that the more possibilities you've listed, the more jobs you'll be able to book.

Think for a while about the lists you've been working on. There's no rush, no compulsion to finish today, and you'll probably do a better job if you take it easy. Think about your lists for several days, particularly the Job Possibilities list that requires your creativity. Mull them over. Sleep on your ideas and see if you can expand on what you have.

Remember that the list process used in the creation of your PMMS is not a one-time thing. Your lists should continue to grow with your music and professional life, and you'll be coming up with new uses for your music as long as you play. The PMMS, if used creatively, should be a long-lasting guide for your music-marketing efforts.

Work Smarter, Not Harder

When you put your Personal Music Marketing System into action by compiling a list of top job prospects, complete with names and addresses, you will probably be surprised at the number of potential clients you develop. For each job category you may have eight or 10 – or as many as 40 or 50 – names of people who need to know about your musical abilities.

One way to keep your work load manageable, and to use your time most efficiently, is to start with the most likely clients, those whose needs closely match your talents. You may end up calling on every single potential client you can think of in every category you've developed, but you'll work smarter if you start with the best prospects.

You have spent time brainstorming, trying to come up with unusual or outlandish ideas for selling your music. Now is the time to go through your lists to pick out the best prospects. Save all your ideas, of course, even the unlikely or impractical ones, but start your efforts where you have the best chance for success.

Match Them Up

Go through both lists now, and see if you can draw any conclusions about your best job possibilities by comparing your personal music inventory with your job ideas lists. First, read back over your personal inventory and note your strong points and most-developed talents. Then, check your Job Possibilities list and note which ones make best use of such strong points. You might put a star by those listings or underline them in red. When that's done, transfer them to the

Best Possibilities Worksheet included in this chapter. You may need to photocopy this page before you start, to be sure of having enough space, or you may want to use a separate notebook. Either way, you're almost ready to start your final list.

For example, if you're a trumpet player, and sight-reading is at the top of your list of well-developed skills, your best job possibilities could include playing shows, work at recording studios, freelancing with local orchestras, and church engagements. You'd want to put those job possibilities at the top of your list. Those won't be your only potential jobs, of course, but you'll be most efficient if you start with the jobs you play best.

Don't discard the idea of playing fanfares at outdoor weddings if that's on your list, but don't make it your top priority, either.

Here's another example. If yours is a chamber-music group, your best job prospects might include educational work at schools, concerts in various places, recording and even society work in homes or at exclusive parties. Thus, you'd rank these as your prime possibilities. Keep all the other ideas for use as you market your music, but plan your efforts to start with the most likely, the best prospects, and work down from there as time permits.

As you rank your Job Possibilities list, looking for the best, most likely prospects, consider several factors. Naturally you'll ask which jobs will pay the best, but you should also think about which will be the least trouble to book and play. Decide which offer year-round opportunity and which are strictly seasonal. Consider which are most common in your area and 'feel right' to you.

Follow the brainstorming techniques discussed earlier, and use the categories on the worksheet to stimulate your own ideas.

If your speciality, for example, is playing Polish music but there isn't a Polish community nearby, you'd be foolish to put Polish weddings at the top of your list. You'll have to temper what you like with what your local market needs.

Don't discard the talent-to-job match-ups that aren't at the top of your list. Later, you'll want to expand your job search beyond your top listings, but it's most efficient to start with your strongest possibilities.

BEST POSSIBILITIES WORKSHEET

Well-Paying Jobs_____

Easy-to-Book Jobs_____

Year-Round Jobs_____

Seasonal Jobs_____

Jobs I'm Already Working_____

Now Add the Names and Numbers

Your refined Best Possibilities should now be ranked in order on the list shown on page 56, with the best prospects for your kind of music at the top, and the rarer, more unusual or even experimental potential jobs listed lower. The reality is that you won't have the time or the energy to call on everybody, so you must be selective.

The final step in developing your Personal Music Marketing System is adding names to each category – finding the prospects' addresses and telephone numbers – and each of your categories may yield dozens of names. If you start with your best prospects, you won't be overwhelmed with the sheer number of sales calls that should be made, and your success ratio will be higher.

Your Good Prospects List

The next list in your Personal Music Marketing System will be all-important to your plan of action. It will contain specific names, addresses and phone numbers of many possible buyers of your music.

Making this list requires a good deal of research, and it will take more time and effort to compile than the other lists. The time you spend finding names and numbers will be very worthwhile, however, because this list will be your blueprint to success in the freelance music business.

The Good Prospects list will be especially useful because it is created with your previous lists as guides. Since those compilations focused closely on the kind of music you do best, your marketing effort will be like a rifle aimed at a very precise target, not like a shotgun blast that would waste your energy searching for clients who don't need your kind of music. The basic sources for names on this list will be:

- Your experience
- The Yellow Pages
- Newspapers and magazines
- Chambers of commerce
- *Kelly's Business Directory* in your library

The names on this final list will be the people you'll call on to sell your music, so the more good prospects you have, the more you'll be able to sell. Your first lists have been general inventories that you compiled by brainstorming and by using ideas from earlier chapters of this book. The Good Prospects list, however, will be specific and will require basic market research to compile.

Categories for All Freelancers

Let's get started on this final list for your PMMS. There are two general categories of prospects that should be on almost all musicians' lists, and we'll start with these. Other, more specialised job prospects will come from your Job Possibilities list. No matter what instrument you play, however, these potential clients should know what you have to offer:

- Booking agents and producers
- Established band-leaders, contractors and conductors, depending on your instrument

Both these categories are important to all freelance players. Even if you think booking agents wouldn't be interested in your Renaissance Music Consortium, there may be a time when a client desperately needs a viola de gamba or a recorder player. *If they don't know you, they won't call you.*

Perhaps the most convenient way to make this list is to use separate sheets of notebook paper for each category and skip a few lines between entries. Remember, paper is cheap. Its cost shouldn't stand in the way of making your list organised and neat. Or you may want to use a separate index card for each potential client.

Maybe you have a computer or some other efficient filing system. Whatever method you use, be sure that you are able to keep up with the information you compile so that you can find and use.it as needed.

Let Your Fingers Do the Walking

You already own one of the main resources that you'll use: the Yellow Pages. This annual compilation of businesses, listed by category, will be invaluable. You couldn't afford to buy the information available to you free in this useful book.

There is a skill to the most effective use of the Yellow Pages, particularly in large cities with huge books. Companies must pay the phone company to be listed in more than one category, so you may have to check several headings before your list is really complete.

Agents and producers, for example, will probably be listed under 'Entertainment agencies' but might also be found under 'Concert agents,' 'Theatrical & variety agents', or several other categories. Be sure, then, to look under each applicable category while you're compiling this list. Use your associating and brainstorming skills to find as many useful categories as you can. Remember, the people who compile the Yellow Pages aren't musicians, so you may have to dig to find the listings you need.

Start your Market Prospects list, then, by going through the Yellow Pages and entering all the booking agents, music producers and band-leaders you can locate. Add recording studios to your list if your playing has reached that level. Include phone numbers and addresses.

Virtually every musician should be known by these people, and you should certainly view booking agents as possible clients, no matter what your instrument. Someday the producer at a recording studio, or a local contractor, will need you, but, to repeat, potential clients don't call you if they don't know you!

Define Your Markets

If you live in a small town, or near a resort area, you'll also want to consult the Yellow Pages for communities near your own. Include all the potential clients within easy driving distance, and remember that it may sometimes be worth your while to drive a few hundred miles for an extra-special job. Your primary market area should include all cities and towns within, say, a hundred miles, and your secondary market area could extend to two or three hundred miles – even further in some cases.

If you play an unusual instrument, or have an uncommon act, you should enlarge your market area so that anyone who needs your rather rare skill will know of your availability. Thus, double-reed players, operatic tenors and harpsichordists will probably define their primary market area more broadly than, say, guitarists or drummers.

A bassoonist can certainly count on less freelance work than a sax player, but the bassoonist will also face less competition, perhaps none. When a recording studio, symphony orchestra, church music director or theatrical group within a hundred miles needs a bassoon, there may be only one choice.

So depending on your area, find Yellow Pages for all your target markets. You can find phone books for other cities at your public library.

Now Expand Your Market List

Once your list contains names of people and groups from the general categories (that is, agents, producers, recording studios and band-leaders), you are ready to start personalising your market list. Now you'll refer to your second compilation, the Job Possibilities list, which contains types of jobs relevant to your music. Still using the Yellow Pages as your primary research tool, go through your Job Possibilities list and find applicable names, addresses and phone numbers for each type of job you are considering.

You may not find many names of individuals, but company names and numbers will do. At first, just locate company names and numbers to match the categories of possible musical jobs from your Job Possibilities list. Later we'll discuss how to find the appropriate contact person at a company.

Watch What Happens

For example, let's say that you are a classical guitarist and that one promising job category in your second list is weddings and receptions. You think that your soothing guitar music could be effectively and profitably used in wedding ceremonies and receptions, and you need to match specific names with this idea. You have the Yellow Pages in hand. Where do you look? In this case, you start with the wedding category. You will probably find:

Wedding services. These include wedding planners, florists, caterers, photographers, video services, car hire firms and reception venues. You can be sure that they are very much into the wedding business, and they should certainly learn of what you can offer their clients.

Some of them keep card files or noticeboards on which you might display your card or promotional literature. In return, offer to recommend *their* services when possible and ask for their cards. You might even want to work out a reciprocal referral or finder's fee arrangement with other business-people in the field. You might send them £20, or even 10 percent of every job you book from their referrals.

Now, follow up by looking under the cross-referenced suggestions for 'Caterers'.

Caterers. Here you'll have to filter through all the listings to find those that specialise in weddings and similar functions. Obviously you should not spend time calling on a fast-food restaurant that lists itself as a caterer, but concentrate on those listings that could be good wedding prospects.

Banqueting rooms. Large restaurants, hotels and meeting halls are listed here. Most hotels will insist on providing the food for affairs held in their facilities, so adding them will not duplicate your 'Caterers' list. Use your discretion, and don' list so many places that you'll be dumbfounded by the number of sales calls to make; list only the most promising prospects.

Florists and photographers. You will probably have noticed many listings fo these businesses in the 'Wedding Services' category, so check these two categories separately in the Yellow Pages. Besides, you'll find several businesses specialising in weddings that were not included elsewhere. Add them to your lis
     You still aren't finished using the Yellow Pages to locate possible clients for your classical guitar playing. Next look at the listings for:

Churches and church halls. You should contact ministers, rabbis, organists and directors of music, especially if you live in a smaller town with fewer caterer and wedding consultants. Since you play classical guitar, you won't be viewed a inappropriate or as competition to the staff organist. You may not get many jobs from these contacts, but you should receive enough referrals to make at least an introductory visit or call worthwhile.

Tent & marquee hire. Many wealthy people hire large, expensive tents for wedding receptions on the lawn. If they can afford to have a party under an expensive tent, they certainly can afford you, so contact the hire companies that provide for these parties. If you are on good terms with them, they'll give you good leads.

Dress hire. Get to know these businesses, and you'll expand your sources of wedding leads and tips. Leave a few of your cards with these companies.

This example should show you how useful the Yellow Pages can be. You'll probably find even more listings for the job categories that interest you, especially if you live in a large city. You are looking for names and numbers to call on, and the Yellow Pages will be a continuing resource. In fact, it might be better to call the Yellow Pages the 'Gold Pages' because they offer so much valuable information.
     You, the classical guitarist in our example, now have numerous specific name on your list all from the Yellow Pages. At this point, you have listed names and numbers for these potential clients:

Booking agents	Caterers
Musical producers	Banqueting rooms
Production companies	Florists
Recording studios	Photographers
Band-leaders	Churches
Wedding planners	Synagogues
Wedding suppliers	Marquees and tents
Dress hire firms	

When you see all these prospects listed, you may feel overwhelmed at the

GOOD PROSPECTS WORKSHEET

	Company	Address	Telephone
Booking Agents			
Music Producers			
Recording Studios			
Band-leaders			
Conference Services			

Add Your Own Headings

number of potential buyers you've found. But just as valuable as any specific wedding lead is the network of referral sources you've discovered.

You've now researched only one category, weddings and receptions, from your Job Possibilities list, but you've found 15 different kinds of job contacts within that one category – probably over a hundred names of individual prospects – just from using the Yellow Pages.

This, then, is the way to find jobs. Do your market research, and you will be astounded at the number of prospects for your music. All it takes is a little work – and you know that many of your competitors are still in bed asleep.

Let Your Fingers Do the Walking, Continued

From the example above, you see that the Yellow Pages can really be a gold mine of job prospects for you. Continue working with this list, the Good Prospects compilation, matching the job-types on it with all the listings you can find in the Yellow Pages. If you are interested in supply teaching, look under 'Schools and Colleges,' 'Nursery Schools,' 'Independent Schools' and 'Music Shops.' If you've listed electronic instrument repair as a strong possibility, check all the listings under 'Music Shops,' 'Musical instrument tuners & repairers,' 'Electronic equipment servicing,' and so on. Be sure to use any cross-references that are given and look in all possible categories for company names and numbers.

With more general categories, such as businesses and public relations firms, you may have to be more selective in what you put on your Good Prospects list. In major cities with large business communities, you'll want to limit your efforts to excellent prospects, – the largest, or the most prosperous, or the best-known, or the most specialised companies in any given field. On the other hand, if you live in a small town or rural area, or if your music is unusual or esoteric, you may have to list every single job possibility you can locate.

In any case, the Yellow Pages will be a continuing and valuable source of job prospects, and you should start your market research with this easy-to-use, always available, and up-to-date source. When you have exhausted the information in the Yellow Pages, you'll probably have more names of potential clients than you could possibly use.

But wait! You have only just begun.

CHAPTER TWELVE

CONTACT PEOPLE

You're making good progress. For your PMMS you've come up with all kinds of interesting ways of playing music for money. You've perhaps actually invented several jobs and thought up parties that just won't work without your own special music. You have your Good Prospects list well under way; it will never be completed, but added to and modified as conditions change in the music world and you gain experience in marketing your music. You're almost ready to activate that Good Prospects list and put it to work for you.

The big question remains. Who will hire you? Who will your clients be? The people you work for will vary, most likely, from a busy mother who's planning a wedding reception to the chief executive of a large corporation. Part of the excitement of the freelance life is that you don't have to do the same thing every day. You welcome the challenge of new jobs, new faces, new clients.

Even so, you'll probably find that much of your work comes through certain well-established channels. It will pay you to get to know these people, understand what they expect, and learn how they operate. You'll be more comfortable, and so will they.

Sometimes it will be appropriate for you to pay a referral or finder's fee to the person who recommends you. Discuss this possibility with those who are in a position to send a lot of business your way. Perhaps you could send a cheque for £20 for each job you book through a particular referral source. Remember that when florists or photographers or party planners recommend you, their reputation is on the line almost as much as yours is. The referral fee is a way of thanking them concretely for having confidence in your work.

As long as you do a good job for the client, a referral fee is perfectly acceptable. However, if the quality of your music is poor, then the referral-fee arrangement becomes suspicious, and the referral may have more to do with the fee than with the quality of the musical product. Be sure that you actually do superior work for the client, and everyone will be happy.

There is a lot of overlapping in these categories, just as there probably is in your own marketing lists. Obviously, a hotel's sales staff will be involved in booking weddings, sales meetings, conventions, and many different functions, and meeting planners will work with conventions, trade shows, annual meetings and other special events.

When you begin to find the same name appearing over and over on your Good Prospects list, make sure that you contact that prospect. And when you make those sales calls, be sure to cover *all* of that prospect's interests. Don't just tell a meeting planner about your great cabaret; also tell her about your dance band, and your dinner music capabilities. Be specific with prospects – and they'll soon be clients.

Prospective Clients

People to contact may fall into many categories. Some are obvious, some less so:

Booking Agents

Booking agents are essentially musical salesmen who make their living by matching clients with the kind of music that's requested. Since agents are so important to most musicians, Chapter 14 discusses them more thoroughly.

Agents take a commission from the client's payment, ranging from 10 to 20 percent. Most booking agencies are small, with a few sales people and a limited clerical staff. Often you'll deal with a one-person agency or with an account executive at a mid-size agency.

Some of these businesses specialise in one kind of entertainment. You should learn which agencies are most likely to need your music and strive for a good relationship with them. However, since virtually every type of musical job discussed in this book can be booked through an agency, it wouldn't hurt for you to know all the agents in your area.

Many large agencies are concerned with famous entertainers and very affluent clients. They may occasionally need small local groups, however, so if you live in a resort area or a busy convention city, you should contact out-of-town agencies to let them know what you can provide. A London agency may book a job in Birmingham, and if it has your promo material, it may hire you directly. Or it may work through a local agency.

Remember, booking agents are not interested in art. Booking agents are interested in money, and the client has it. When you talk to agents, emphasise what you can do to make clients happy. Most agents are more interested in your entertainment sense than your perfect pitch.

Convention Planners

Businesses that plan conventions are common in large cities that host many conventions, and they try to provide a complete service to their clients. They arrange transport, food, lodging, tours – and entertainment. If you can meet the regular needs of the convention industry for hospitality, dinner, dance and cabaret music, you'll find that convention planners will rely on you.

Many such companies are local and small, serving regular clients. They may book music directly or work through an entertainment agency. Sometimes, tour companies will expand to provide convention service. These people know far ahead of time who's coming to town, when, and for how long; the type of programme being planned; and the possibilities for using music. You'll soon discover that most, but not all, convention work is booked through agents, and you'll learn which agents need your constant attention.

If you can make helpful suggestions during the planning stage (which will be months or years before the meeting), you'll find that your ideas are welcomed. Convention planners and booking agents can get into ruts, too, and your innovative suggestions, especially if they relate to the theme or location of the meeting, can result in more work for you. Note, please, that this applies to practically all convention events needing music. Present your ideas and suggestions early enough to be acted on.

Some planners will add your fees into their overall charge to the client and pay you as a sub-contractor. Others will simply refer you to the client and have you make your own contractual arrangements. In this case, you may want to pay a 'finder's fee' to the person who refers the job to you.

Caterers

Busy caterers know more about the social scene in a community than almost anyone else, so stay in touch with them. Often, a caterer will have a years-long association with a wealthy family, or a company, and plan all its party needs, from flowers to entertainment.

If you can become well known to the established caterers in your area, you're apt to get many job leads. Even if your music is out of the ordinary, a creative catering company might very well need it for an unusual kind of party.

Catering companies can be large and well-established, with permanent facilities and large staffs, or they can be small family operations with little capital. Many caterers operate out of their homes and rent all the necessary equipment for each job. Some specialise in one kind of event – wedding receptions, for example. Get to know them all, and offer to pay a referral fee for leads that result in jobs.

Wedding Services

If your kind of music lends itself to weddings, you'll need to know the people in your community who are in the wedding business. Many photographers, florists, formal-wear shops and consultants make most of their income from weddings.

Wedding consultants, who are at the centre of all this activity, often recommend musicians to prospective brides and grooms. If they can recommend you with confidence, you'll have a valuable resource for finding work.

These consultants are often one-person companies, frequently working from home. You'll find them under 'Wedding Services' in the Yellow Pages. Many large department stores, formal-wear shops, florists and photographers also offer wedding-planning services, so include them in your list.

Remember that the wedding consultant business is built, like your own, on referrals and on reputation. If you do a good job, you'll find lots of work from this source. If you aren't dependable, though, or don't play appropriate music, wedding consultants will delete you from their referral lists. When you take a job through a referral, remember that not only is *your* reputation on the line, but also that of the person who recommended you. Do your best to uphold his or her faith in you.

Businesses

This is a large category that includes both small, owner-operated companies and the largest companies in the country. What they have in common is that they use music for certain specific purposes, and that they are interested mostly in the 'bottom line.'

When you deal with small businesses, you'll talk directly to the owner or the manager, and it's usually pretty clear what kind of music is needed and who you have to please. If the person who hires you is also the person who writes the cheque, you know who the boss is.

Many large companies have their own staff of meeting planners. These people may be in charge of all the company's functions, from elegant receptions to huge shareholders' meetings.

Establishing contacts within some large companies is difficult, even challenging. The person who hires you is often an office junior or a lower-level manager; as a result, you have the problem of figuring out not only what your immediate contact wants, but what his or her boss wants as well. In many company settings, office politics are overwhelmingly important, and you usually don't know who the players are. Furthermore, many people with different musical tastes and entertainment preferences may have to be pleased: the person who hired you, his or her superior, and, not infrequently, several more levels of bosses.

So, when the 27-year-old junior executive who hired you to play current hits tells you at a company dance to start playing Glen Miller, it may really be the 78-year-old chairman of the company who issued the order. The junior executive's ultimate interest is in making his top boss happy.

Sales meetings may be planned by a vice-chairman or director in charge of sales. When large companies are trying to motivate their sales forces, it sometimes seems that money is no object. One well-known computer company refers, for instance, to its sales meeting expenditures as 'dumping money.' Take care, then, that you don't *underprice* your music. You can always bargain downward. Some companies don't feel that they are getting their money's worth unless the bill is high!

Another financial point you should understand when pricing your music for large businesses is that many companies prefer to spend lavishly on business meetings and company events rather than pay the money in taxes. Do your best to help.

Get to know the meeting-planning staffs of all the large companies based in your area. You may be surprised at the range of occasions for which they need music. Businesses entertain in much the same way as individuals do, just on a larger scale, and their meeting planning staff can be a valuable contact for you.

Associations

Many associations have a professional staff of meeting planners, and you should call on them if they're in your community. Some groups will rely on volunteers from the membership, and you'll need to locate the secretary of the entertainment committee to offer your services. Other contacts will be the same as those discussed under 'conventions.'

Civic, Social, and Non-profit Organisations

A few civic groups have full-time managers for their meeting places, and you should call on them. Other organisations are run by committees of members; let them know what you can offer. Watch the newspaper for information about these events. File names and dates for next year's sales calls if you're too late this year. Many non-profit organisations have permanent fund-raising staffs; contact the director in your area.

Government Jobs

Find out if your county has a cultural-affairs office or something similar. If so, get

in touch, and find out what they do. Also, contact your local regional arts
association, and determine its involvement in producing special festivals and fairs.
Your local tourist board probably publishes a detailed calendar of special events,
including sponsors' names and addresses. The reference section of your local
library can help you locate sources of grant, loan or scholarship money.

Nightclub Jobs

Usually the club owner or manager hires musicians, though some clubs have a
music director. Larger clubs and hotels often hire exclusively through an agency,
and bands may rotate on a company circuit. Some agencies work exclusively
with nightclubs and book only certain kinds of bands, so try to find agencies
whose specialities match yours. Current demo tapes will be helpful, and you'll
have to audition to book many club jobs. Up-to-date promo material, including
recent photos and reviews of your group, will also impress club owners and
managers.

Restaurant Jobs

Usually you'll deal with the owner or manager to book jobs in restaurants. Some
chains or larger establishments have entertainment directors, often musicians
themselves. Of course, booking agents frequently handle placement of musicians
in these positions, and private parties will often hire their own entertainment or
rely on the restaurateur's suggestions.

Hotel Music

Staff turnover in many hotels is high, so your carefully cultivated contact person
may suddenly disappear – or turn up at another hotel. You'll need to stay in
touch with entertainment directors, catering and sales staffs, and, in smaller
properties, the general manager. Occasionally, there will be an entertainment
director, usually a band-leader, who books all the hotel's musical needs. Often, of
course, hotels deal exclusively with entertainment agencies. Private parties and
conventions frequently book their own music independently of the hotel.

Deputising

Normally, the musician for whom you are depping will hire you directly;
occasionally, however, the band-leader, or even the booking agency will call you
for work as a replacement. Stay in touch with musicians, and be sure you are
listed with your local union branch as being available.

Public Relations and Advertising

Contact specific account executives at advertising and PR firms to suggest music
for particular events. Each executive is usually in charge of several projects, and
will welcome your input. If you are making a 'get acquainted' call without
specific suggestions in mind, try to see as many creative directors and account
executives as possible so they'll know what you have to offer for their future
projects.

Remember that most jingles and recorded commercials are developed by
advertising agency people, so if you are a writer or arranger, you'll want to make
this a prime market.

Fashion Shows

To book fashion-show engagements, talk with modelling and entertainment agencies, and publicity departments or the buyers at department stores, boutiques and merchandise marts. Often, shopping malls, country clubs and large restaurants will sponsor their own fashion shows, so stay in touch with their entertainment directors and publicity people. Occasionally, schools and other non-profit organisations will sponsor annual fund-raising shows.

Clubs

To book club engagements, see the club manager or social-activities director. Some clubs are run by committees, so you'll call on them. Special events are often planned by temporary committees or appointed directors. Many organisations have a social committee, and you should contact its chairman or chairwoman to offer your services. Since the people handling organisational activities often change each year, you'll have to update your list of contact names frequently.

Private Parties

To locate and book parties in homes, you'll need to become well-known to the influential party-givers in your area. You can contact them directly from notices in the society pages of your local paper or indirectly through booking agencies, caterers, party-supply hire companies or florists. This is an area where word-of-mouth advertising works best, so build your reputation and freely hand out your cards to likely prospects.

Shows

Large road shows usually book local players through a contractor, leader or agency. Theatres have music directors or committes. To find work at theatres, talk to the director, producer or musical director. To book your own show, contact agents and meeting planners, convention consultants, and other musicians.

Circuses and Travelling Shows

Road shows like the circus will usually carry a few key players and a conductor and pick up other musicians locally. Stay in contact with leaders and contractors for this work. You may be able to book yourself directly, particularly if you have a strong, entertaining act.

Tourist-Related Jobs

To suggest and book tourist-related jobs, see the entertainment directors of tour-promotion outfits, tourist attractions, botanical gardens, and other local attractions. Also call on convention planners and the entertainment committees of local civic clubs and associations. Booking agents, of course, need to know of your abilities and ideas, as do cruise lines.

Orchestral Jobs

Orchestral jobs usually demand auditions, notices of which are published in the national press and posted on music-department noticeboards. The conductor of local amateur orchestras may hire extra personnel, and knowing the teachers and classical players in your community can lead to jobs.

Church and Synagogue Work

For freelance church/synagogue work, stay in touch with the permanent staff. Full-time positions may be filled by church committees or denominational boards, and ads for vacant positions will be found in organ and church music publications.

Schools

For peripatetic instrumental teaching, contact the office of your LEA Music Advisor. Contact independent schools direct.

School and University Reunions

The administrative offices of schools, colleges and universities can direct you to the planning committee for each year's reunion. Once again, you'll be dealing with a committee that may know nothing about booking bands, so part of your job will be educational. Since committees change for each reunion year, stay in touch with the relevant office to locate specific contacts for each group.

Teaching

To find students for private music teaching, contact other teachers for referrals (particularly if your speciality is different from theirs). Also, let local band and choral directors and school music teachers know what you have to offer. Church music directors may be able to send you students, and so can music shops. Some large music shops offer instruction on their premises, and some cities have privately run schools of music that use part-time instructors. Many music shops will let you display promotional material on their noticeboards, and small ads in the Yellow Pages or local newspapers will be effective.

Technical Assistance

Roadies, sound-people and technical assistants are usually hired by the bands they serve. If the band has a manager, he or she will be the one to see. Be sure that you are known as a technically proficient musician at local studios, music shops, rehearsal rooms and equipment-hire firms. Concert halls and nightclubs also use sound specialists, so you should stay in touch with them as well as with sound-reinforcement companies.

Repair Work

Technical jobs are found in music shops, electronic repair shops, and factory service centres. Many department stores or music shops offer employment to piano tuners and repair technicians. Frequently, this work is done by independent craftsmen who own their own businesses, so contact both large and small repair services.

Writing, Arranging and Copying

To sell your writing and copying talents, become known at recording studios, ad agencies, music colleges and even music shops in your area. Be sure that the Musicians Union has your name on file.

Recording Work

To become a frequent player on recording sessions, you'll need to be known by producers and engineers at all the studios in your area – and by writers and arrangers. Other players may recommend you, or advertising agencies that know your talents may request that you be hired to play a session.

Your range of clients is likely to be very broad. You'll probably deal with a wide variety of business-people, teachers, brides, concert promoters, park managers, public-relations professionals, advertising agencies, and many others as your career grows.

As discussed at the beginning of this book, the key to success in dealing with a large variety of contacts is to remember that for each different client you must faithfully provide the kind of music that he or she explicitly hires you to produce. Find out exactly what the client wants, and do your best to provide it.

Many times you'll have the difficult task of dealing with entertainment committees. A company Christmas party, for example, may be planned by a group made up of people ranging from the car park attendant to the chief executive. Your job is to try to please them all. In making presentations to such a diverse group, emphasise your versatility and explain that you are accustomed to dealing with mixed ages, backgrounds and musical tastes.

In every case, with every client, your ultimate task as a freelance musician is to do what the job requires. That may not be easy, but it will ensure a happy client – and a growing career.

Making Contact

Use your sales skills and ingenuity to reach the right person, the one who buys music. Sometimes your contact will be obvious, sometimes not. Perhaps you'd like to book your band at an annual company dinner-dance. Who do you call?

Simply call the receptionist and ask for the person who's in charge of planning that event. Often that's all it takes, because that person is looking for you, too, even though he or she may not know it yet. If the receptionist connects you with the wrong person, explain what you are doing and ask to be referred to the right extension.

Telephone manners are very important in making contact with potential clients. Identify yourself clearly, and once you've established that you're talking to the person who will be planning the event, say, "I'd like to talk to you about music for your dinner-dance. Is this a good time, or should I call back later?" Never jump right into your sales pitch without this basic courtesy.

You may experience some difficulty in reaching the person you need to talk-to in a large company, for many secretaries and receptionists are trained to protect their bosses from interruptions and unknown callers. Be prepared to answer the question, "What company are you with?" If your freelance business has a name, state it confidently. Since a company name can be more impressive in the business world than your own, you might wish to consider calling your enterprise something like Upbeat Music, Mary Willis Studio, Melodies Unlimited or High-Tech Productions.

If you haven't chosen a name for your freelance enterprise, don't fake it. That is, don't make up a name for one-time use. Just tell the receptionist that you're a professional musician calling Mr. Jones to offer your services for the dinner-dance XYZ Company is planning. The secretary probably knows about the dinner-dance, and she'll know that Mr. Jones needs to hire musicians. By being forthright, you'll often be able to get right through to the person you need to talk to.

You may, on the other hand, experience 'the runaround,' whereby the first secretary says, "Oh, I think Mrs. Brown's office handles that sort of thing." Then Mrs. Brown's receptionist says, "Perhaps you need to talk with our recreational director," who, it turns out, arranges inter-departmental tennis matches, but hasn't the slightest idea about hiring musicians. Keep cool, remain courteous. Somewhere in the business bureaucracy you'll get what you want, if you politely ask for help from someone with a particularly friendly voice.

At times, you'll be amazed at widespread incompetence. Occasionally, you'll even run across arrogance and rudeness. The key is to keep trying, and remember that you are offering something that potential clients *need*. You're not just wasting their time.

When you have reached the person who is actually in charge of planning the event in question, or hiring the band, it's usually a good idea to try to set up a meeting. Business-people are used to meeting clients, and will want to size you up. Use the ideas in Chapter 15, 'Selling,' to make them want to hire you.

Before the meeting, you'll find it useful to send your publicity material to the prospective client, along with a short note thanking him or her for talking to you and confirming the time of your sales call. Unfortunately, many business-people are basically suspicious of musicians – and vice versa – so a preliminary meeting can be very useful in getting to know each other.

Maintain your Who's Important file as discussed in Chapter 4, so that all the information you've worked hard to gather is available when you need it. You'll never be able to recall all the essential personal and business details if you don't write them down for quick retrieval. Think of your memory as an untrustworthy, temporary file. Use your Who's Important file as a reliable, permanent means for helping maintain good working relationships with contacts and clients.

Your network of contacts and clients should grow with your career – but it won't if you fail to nurture it. Prospective clients will forget you if you don't keep in touch through gentle reminders of your availability. Former clients may not think of you unless you keep your name in circulation.

There is nothing wrong with asking clients to help further your career and broaden your network of contacts by writing letters of commendation for jobs particularly well done. There is nothing wrong, either, with asking your best clients to recommend you to others. Personal recommendations, written or by word of mouth, are probably the best kind of advertising. Most people familiar with your work will be happy to suggest you to their friends and colleagues who need music. Try to make them feel that by passing your name along they'll be doing their friends – as well as you – a favour. Be sure, of course, that you express your appreciation to everyone who helps your career in this way.

Cultivate your clients. Tap into professional and social networks to expand your base of operation. Above all, keep the lines of communication to all contacts busy, but don't overload them. Unobtrusive persistence is the name of this game.

CHAPTER THIRTEEN

MORE MARKET RESEARCH

Now your Good Prospects list is well under way from your research in the Yellow Pages. That will be one of your main sources of ideas, names and addresses, but there are other market-research tools that will help your prospects list grow and stay current.

You should keep your market research active throughout your career. Just because you have a couple of hundred names as excellent prospects doesn't mean you can stop working and relax. You must keep up with changes in your community and in the music business.

Are You Experienced?

Your list should certainly include all the clients for whom you have worked in the past. This means other musicians, agents and clients themselves. Every business-person knows that past clients are also the best prospects. *But don't let this mislead you into thinking only of the same old jobs.* Your entire marketing effort is to discover *new clients* and develop *new needs* for your music. So use your past music work as a base, a starting point for expansion.

As you add past clients' names to your Good Prospects list, use the brainstorming and association techniques described earlier to develop new names. Look for similar people who might need your music. Thus, if you have played for the opening of a new bank building for Nat West, add other banks to your list. If Nat West needed your music, why can't Barclays and Lloyds use you too? If your barbershop quartet has entertained the local bar association at its annual dinner/dance, add other professional groups to your list – associations of doctors, dentists, psychologists, psychiatrists, accountants, engineers. Similar groups have similar needs and will respect your credentials.

Use your past clients list in three ways:

- As a core listing of people who have used your music in the past and are likely to need it again. Be sure to keep them up on what you have to offer.
- As a mental springboard for coming up with other, similar prospects.
- As a source of recommendations. When you have played an exceptionally good engagement, it may be appropriate for you to solicit a letter of recommendation from the client for your files. Later, as you prepare publicity material, a few quotes (or even entire letters) will be very effective.

Newspapers

To keep abreast of current activities in your community, read the local papers. These provide valuable, up-to-date information.

A newspaper will keep you informed about events that use music, and you should read it every day. The only disadvantage is that the lead time may be too short; the music may have already been arranged by the time the newspaper publishes its story. If this happens with a recurring event such as an annual dance, cut out the article and put it in your memo file for the following year. Then make your first contact eight or nine months before the job. It's better to act too soon than too late.

You will find that the most useful newspapers are the local ones. Here are some ways to use your local paper to find situations that could use your music. Again, you'll want to use your Job Possibilities list as a guide.

Weddings, parties and social events will be covered in the 'Society,' 'Women' or 'Lifestyle' sections. If you are trying to book weddings and receptions, you'll find leads from the engagement announcements, though you'll need to act quickly. Also, people who are frequently mentioned in the gossip columns as party-givers certainly need to know who you are.

Notice which country clubs are planning special events and which clubs are most active or about to expand. You might learn of the existence of a new social club through newspaper reading.

Watch the 'Social Events' calendar for dances and parties to be given by community, social and church organisations. Again, while the music may already be booked when the newspaper story appears, you should cut out the article, put it in your next year's file, and contact the client six to eight months in advance.

The 'Business' section will alert you to all kinds of activities that might benefit from your music. You'll find coverage of forthcoming grand openings, new-product launches, and special promotions. You'll need to move fast in order to book music for these events.

Watch for stories about coming conventions, trade shows, sales meetings and product promotions. You may find hints about special sales that have specific music tie-ins, or seasonal business activities such as new-car launches that need your music. You'll also find leads concering executive promotions and retirements, both of which can result in parties that need music.

Pay special attention to any columns that cover business personalities in your area. You'll find important contact names, such as the public-relations firm handling a political campaign, or a newly hired catering director at a major hotel, or a developer planning a new resort for the nearby seaside. Your alertness should provide extra leads.

By reading the business section, you may even find news that you would expect to hear through the musical grapevine but may not. You could learn of a new recording studio in town, of a new restaurant/cabaret, or plans for a street festival to revive part of the inner city.

The Arts and Leisure section will yield news of forthcoming concerts, newly formed chamber music groups, auditions for local orchestras and theatrical productions, recitals and nightclub appearances. Your music could be needed in many of these stations. You should keep up with who's doing what and what's going on in the local musical community.

You may learn, for instance, that the city's symphony orchestra is putting on a series of school concerts to demonstrate the instruments of the orchestra and introduce the students to classical music.

You could apply this idea to your own kind of music, be it pop, jazz or medieval church music, and explore the possibility of obtaining a grant or other support for a similar kind of school concert programme. The possibilities are almost limitless if you keep your imagination active and keep up with what others are doing. Often, by making a slight change, you can apply an idea to your own situation. When you get a good idea, it doesn't matter if it's original – as long as you act on it.

The 'Religion' or 'Church' section will alert you to special musical events and programmes, many of which need professional musical help. If you are too late for this year's performance, make a note to contact the musical or choral director for next year's events. Holiday seasons will be particularly active. Also note which churches have the most dynamic music programmes, and be aware of how your music might fit in.

The 'Sports' pages will keep you up-to-date on athletic events and tournaments that may employ music for awards banquets and dances.

The papers you read may or may not have a separate 'Education' section, but every newspaper carries stories about education – institutions which are particularly active in promoting ethnic and folk music, which college is expanding its concert programme and so on.

You might get an idea using your music in hospital therapy from a feature about that subject. A story about street musicians or a singing telegram service in another city could inspire you to apply that notion to your own area.

The paper will also help you stay abreast of cultural trends, fads and changes, and you can direct your career more accurately if you know what is going on. Society is constantly evolving, and the music business changes every day. The static person will soon be left behind.

By keeping up with society's trends, you may be among the first to know that disco is coming in – or going out. You may be able to profit from a new interest in jazz, or folk, or ethnic music. You may need to know about new ways to apply computers to the teaching of improvisation. You could benefit from reading about midday concerts in local parks if you apply that idea to your own situation.

And don't forget that the 'Classified' section is a great source for buying and selling instruments and other musical equipment.

In short, a close reading of the local newspaper will prove directly beneficial to most musicians Read it with a pair of scissors handy, maintain a file of cuttings, and add important names to your Good Prospects list. A thorough and imaginative daily reading of the newspaper can make the subscription pay for itself many times over.

Again, it's better to act too early than too late, so make notes in your memo file six, eight even 10 months in advance for annual events. If there is lots of competition for a particular job, you might even contact the prospect a full year ahead with your introductory visit.

Don't Forget The Ads!

Don't overlook the ads. Much time, thought and money is spent producing them, and you can find out a lot about your area by paying attention to what is being advertised. Perhaps a new hotel is touting its Sunday morning brunch. If the atmosphere is formal, couldn't it use a string quartet? Or if it's informal, wouldn't a jazz trio or folk-singer be appropriate?

Maybe a local manufacturer is promoting a new line of garden furniture. You might call on the public relations or advertising department to suggest an early spring display featuring your big band at a local shopping centre to introduce the new products.

Use magazine and newspaper ads as *idea producers*. You probably don't need a lift truck or a multi-terminal computer system, but if those items are prominently advertised, you could probably find a tie-in for your music. When businesses are spending big money promoting products, let them know how you can help.

When you think like a business-person, you'll realise that music can be very useful in creating a mood or generating excitement, and you'll begin to notice all the kinds of events that your music could help. Newspapers and magazines will provide a continuing source of these ideas for your Good Prospects list. You'll find that reading current periodicals can be just as important to your career as reading music.

Chambers of Commerce

Chambers of commerce can be very useful sources of information to freelance musicians. These organisations promote business activity in your area, and you can learn a lot by using their services.

Chambers of commerce try to promote all kinds of business activity, including conventions. They can provide helpful information about economic activity in your area and can alert you to new industry, community celebrations and events, company expansions, and other occurences that might need your music. Often, local chambers publish newsletters or calendars of events that you'll find useful.

If you perform a show featuring the life and works of a local composer, you may find that the chamber of commerce will even be interested in promoting *you*.

Library Resources

As you continue to find good prospects to match the entries on your Job Possibilities list, be aware of the aid that your local library can give. Librarians, especially those who work in reference departments, have access to unbelievable amounts of information, and you'll find them to be very helpful as you do your market research.

Here are a few ways you can use the library:

- Get to know the *Directory of British Associations* and *Trade Associations & Professional Bodies of the UK,* both of which will be in the reference department. These are valuable books listing all the associations in the UK. Two further publications may also be useful: *Centres and Bureaux* and *Councils, Committees and Boards,* also available in the reference section.
- Your library may subscribe to magazines that list forthcoming conventions around the country. Ask the librarian.
- The library probably has out-of-town telephone books from nearby cities. You will find these useful – particularly the Yellow Pages.

- Many libraries maintain a local history collection. If you are producing a show with local or historical interest, or if you are looking for information to use in preparing a sales call, these files could be a gold mine. Always ask the librarians for help; you'll save time because they know exactly where to look for all kinds of information.
- Don't forget that books can be very helpful in many ways. For example, before you start making sales calls, you will probably want to read one of the excellent books on sales techniques. Also, to keep up with changes in the tax laws, you can find a current handbook on tax preparation for the self-employed.

Your Personal Music Marketing System is Shaping Up

Your Good Prospects list should be quite substantial now that you've researched the information sources discussed in this chapter. Devise reminders to consult these sources routinely: newspapers every day, magazines each issue, the Yellow Pages at least every new edition, chambers of commerce every three months or so, and the local library depending on how fast it acquires new publications.

You may already have so many names on your Good Prospects list that you can't call on all the people included, but what a problem to have! At least you've proved that you don't have to limit yourself to the same old jobs for the same old clients.

In every community there are many job opportunities for freelance musicians, and the simple market research sources discussed in this chapter will help you find them. If you use these sources to keep up with developments in your community, you'll probably be playing a stimulating variety of jobs as often as you'd like.

Finding jobs is probably your most important task as a freelance musician. You can proceed in a hit-or-miss fashion, as most of your competitors will, and be satisfied with more of the same old thing. Or you can use your Personal Music Marketing System to locate jobs that are matched to your talents, *jobs that need your music.*

It takes a little work, but it's worth it.

CHAPTER FOURTEEN

WORKING
WITH AGENTS

Many musicians just want to play music. They know little or nothing about the business side of music or about booking jobs. For such musicians, agents can be very important. In fact, many players book most or all of their work through agencies and never worry about dealing directly with clients.

As this book has shown, however, finding jobs that can use your kind of music is not too difficult, and most musicians can profitably locate work on their own.

Perhaps there aren't any booking agents in your community, or your kind of music is so uncommercial that agents aren't interested. Or perhaps you just like the business aspects of the profession. In these cases, you'll certainly be your own agent, use your PMMS, and pay yourself the commission.

Actually, of course, it's not an either/or situation. Most freelance players work with agents sometimes and book jobs directly on other occasions.

One of the 'universal markets' that should be at the top of your Good Prospects list is a listing of all the agents in your community. Even if you do most of your work through your own direct dealings with clients, you need to know, and be known by, booking agents.

Many musicians, particularly those with a little business acumen, resent the agent's role. They ask, "Why should that non-musician get a cut of the money I earn?" Nevertheless, you need agents for two basic reasons. One is that in many areas, particularly large cities, agents control much of the work. Major hotels, for instance, will sign exclusive agreements with booking agents, and all the work for that hotel goes through the agent. If you don't know the agent, you don't get the work.

The second reason that you should work with agents is that they're specialists. Their business is selling music and entertainment, and they should be expert sales-people with highly developed skills. Matching your musical talent with a good agent's sales abilities can result in a potent combination that will be profitable to both of you.

Establishing a Good Relationship

Musicians play for many reasons – including fun, artistic expression and personal satisfaction – but agents are in it for the money. Most agents are 99.9 percent business-people, interested in the bottom line. Like other clients, they don't care about your musical soul; they only want to know if they can make money with your music. So you should think of them as you think of other clients, and find ways to demonstrate that your music will fill their needs. They must believe that your talent will make money for them when they use their sales skills to find jobs for you.

You get best results by finding booking agencies that handle your kind of music and match your temperament and your way of doing business. Some agencies are completely rock/pop oriented, some book only college concerts, some specialise in Jewish weddings and other ethnic functions, and others book primarily large shows for major conventions. Some specialise in the nightclub circuit, while others mainly book travelling shows for armed-forces installations around the world. Other agencies promote superstar-level classical soloists and chamber groups. The variety is as wide as the spectrum of music, and you will have to shop around to find an agent who books the kind of freelance jobs you're looking for.

You should also spend a little time becoming known at agencies whose focus is not on your speciality, because occasionally they may need you. For example, an agency that books primarily rock bands for college dances and parties may sometimes get a call for a harpist to play a wedding ceremony. The agency won't turn down the business just because harp music isn't its speciality, so if that's your instrument, and you have let this agency know of your existence, you'll probably get the job.

The task of finding an agent or agents who will serve you well is already under way. You're well into the search, that is, if you've already compiled your Good Prospects list instead of waiting to do it after reading this book straight through. You still have to determine, of course, which agents would be interested in selling your music – and which ones you'd like to work with.

Once you have found an agency, or several, that will work with you, the following guidelines will help you create and maintain a good relationship:

- Communicate honestly and clearly with any booking agencies you plan to work with. Let them know *exactly* what you can and cannot do. Don't take a job if it is beyond your capabilities or outside your area of competence. You'll only hurt yourself, and the agency won't hire you again.
- Discuss details with any agency you work for. Be sure that you understand where the job is, what time it begins and ends, what dress is appropriate, whether you must take your own piano and sound equipment, how much the job pays, who to report to, whether you must use the goods entrance at the back of the hotel, what time rehearsal is, whether you are to play alto or tenor sax – or both – how much you'll be paid for overtime, who authorises overtime, and so on. Often, small details make a job successful, and this aspect of the music business should not be treated lightly. Your agent is a go-between for you and the client, and you must pay close attention to be sure that all the details are covered, understood and agreed upon. Try to have a contract or a written letter confirming these important points.
- You may need to use your musical expertise to advise agents. Sometimes, in the heat of a sales call, an agent will promise the moon, but *you* will be on the hot seat if you can't deliver. Don't let an agent sell your five-piece rock band as a jazz ensemble or your 16-piece big band as a soul revue.
- *Never ever* try to 'steal' a client from an agent. When you play a job that an agent has booked, you should refer any inquiries generated by that job to the

agent. Never hand out your own card at an agent-booked job; carry a few cards from the agency. Good agents work very hard to find and book jobs, and you'll quickly find yourself black-listed if you try to go around them to book yourself direct with their clients.

(This does not mean that you shouldn't try to book yourself when no written or implied agreement with an agent is compromised. Just don't try to steal clients who 'belong' to your agent.)

- Always have a clear understanding with the agency about money. Is the price quoted net to you, or does the agency's commission come out of it? Will the client pay the agent direct, or should you pick up a cheque? Will the agent pay you immediately following the job, or will you have to wait weeks or even months until the agent has been paid by the client? If the worst happens and the client doesn't pay, will the agent pay you anyway? Or if the job is cancelled two days before the performance, will you be paid?

Misunderstandings about money have ruined many relationships between musicians and booking agents. If you have a firm, clear – better yet, *written* – understanding about these matters with your agent, you'll both be happier and more prosperous.

Love-Hate is Here to Stay

Usually, the basis for tension between musicians and their agents is that they are trying to do very different things. At the simplest level, the difference in what the agent wants and what the musician wants cannot be reconciled. The best you can do is understand it and know where your agent's loyalty lies.

Musicians want to play, to play as well as they can, and to derive as much personal satisfaction as they can from their performances. Perhaps making money is part of the goal, but it's not always first on the list. Many musicians' allegiance is, essentially, to their music, their art and their craft.

Agents, on the other hand, are business-people whose loyalty is with their hard-earned clients. Their principal interest is in maintaining those clients and their business. When there is a musician-client conflict, the agent will *automatically* take the client's side, right or wrong. Why? Because that's where the money comes from. Musicians can easily be replaced, but if a client goes to another agency, that account, and its revenue, is lost.

By accepting the reality of this basic difference in orientation, you'll save yourself a lot of misapprehension and unpleasantness. Regardless of what they tell you, agents represent their paying clients – not you, unless you're a star or celebrity – and their aim is to keep those clients satisfied. Don't be shocked. That's their job.

So, at a convention where you're providing walk-up and awards music before playing for a dance, don't be surprised if the agent – on behalf of the client – asks you not to take a break but to play for two and a half hours non-stop. If that's what the client wants, that's what the agent wants.

All this doesn't mean, of course, that agents are your enemies. It's just that if you understand what the bottom line really is, you can avoid needless conflict and make your relationship more productive.

It Takes Money to Make Money

Why are agents entitled to part of your money? Simply because they've earned it, doing things that you may not know how to do or may dislike doing. Besides, a good agent is an expert sales-person, and can probably sell your talents better than you can.

There are various reasons that an agent should – in fact, *must* – get a percentage of the total.

If your agent, Mark Smithers, has an office, then his overheads are much higher than yours. He has to pay substantial rent and services. His ad in the Yellow Pages may cost several hundred pounds a year. The installation cost for a business phone is considerably more than that of a domestic phone, and the monthly charges are much higher. Nobody gives him letterheads, envelopes, invoices, typewriters, adding machines, computers, petrol, business lunches or insurance. His office fax and photocopy machines probably cost him two thousand pounds.

If Mark has a staff, his book-keeping load is enormous, with national and local regulations to comply with and licences and taxes to pay. He must hire an accountant to deal with his tax affairs. He must hire a secretary to type letters proposing your services to clients. He must hire, and probably train, sales-people to sell your musical services to clients.

And Mark may spend a hundred pounds in long-distance phone calls, business lunches and postage trying to book your group for a job, only to lose the business to a competitor who quoted a slightly lower price. In short, it may cost even a small agency *three or four thousand pounds a month* just to keep the office running.

The cost of doing business is high, and your agent, who finds work for you, deserves the percentage that he gets. Thank him. Don't begrudge him his fee. Much of the work Mark finds for you is work you'd never otherwise get, so you are gaining, not losing by using his services.

Unfortunately, there are shady agents. Usually, their poor reputations will warn you to be careful. Stay away from the ones who don't pay promptly or don't pay the agreed-upon amount. Avoid those whose jobs cancel frequently or who don't abide by standard agreements. One bad experience with a booking agency should warn you to watch your step. Two such experiences should end your relationship. Most booking agents, however, especially the established ones who prosper, are hardworking and honest business-people who need your music as much as you need their sales talent.

Long-Term Agreements

What should you do if Mark, your agent, wants you to sign an exclusive contract so that all your performances and self-promotions must be booked through him? For most freelance musicians, this situation won't arise, but possibly an agent or producer will promise lots of money if you will sign an exclusive contract.

Find a lawyer with experience in entertainment. *Never* sign a long-term contract with an agent, producer or recording company without having *your* lawyer check it over.

It may be that an exclusive agreement would, in fact, be a great thing for you and for the agency. But it might be a very bad idea, because if you have no way out of a one-sided contract, you could be out of luck.

If an agent wants to be your exclusive representative, you must know if you are *guaranteed* a certain amount of work, or money, or publicity. Don't sign a contract on the basis of good intentions, excellent prospects, or even years of friendship. With your lawyer's help, consider:

● Does the exclusive contract require the agent to book you a certain number of jobs for a specified rate of pay? Or does it just require him to try?
● What if an old college friend wants you to play for her wedding, free? Would your exclusive contract force you to pay the agency a commission on your own gift to a friend?
● What if your record doesn't sell as well as expected? Is the producer or record company still obliged to spend a certain amount of money and effort on publicity and advertising?
● What if you break your arm and can't play the planned series of concerts? Could you be liable for your agent's lost profits?
● What if the planned series of concerts fizzles out? Will you be released from the contract if the promoter fails to deliver the promised crowds?
● What if clients approach you directly? Will you be obliged to pay a commission to the agency from your profits? This is not an uncommon problem for freelance players, but careful planning will help you avoid it.

These are a few of the kinds of questions that should be *legally* settled, *to your lawyer's satisfaction,* before you sign any long-term agreement. It's not that you should mistrust those who show an interest in your career. It's just that agents, producers, promoters and record companies are primarily looking out for themselves. That is not the same thing as looking out for you. You'll have to do that yourself.

Good Teamwork Can Pay Off

Establishing a good relationship with all the appropriate agents in your area can be an excellent first step for you. You need to work a lot of jobs, and the professional sales staff of a dynamic agency can help you meet your goal. As your musical life expands, be sure to keep these agencies updated about your new abilities, repertory and equipment. They need to know what you have to sell.

Don't ignore the big agencies. Even if they don't have offices in your area, they may occasionally need to provide music for a client in your town. Put them on your brochure mailing list so that when they need your kind of talent in your area, they'll know who to call.

The teamwork between a good musician and a good agent can be very productive, with each person doing what he or she knows (and likes) best. When you work through an honest, hard-working agency, you'll find that music and business aren't incompatible after all.

CHAPTER FIFTEEN

SELLING

Must you – yourself – sell your music?

Yes. You won't make any money until someone – a client, an agent or another musician – pays you to play. You must convince someone to hire you, and that's selling.

You may protest that you're a musician and not a salesman, but selling is not as difficult or intimidating as you probably think. You have focused your PMMS on people who are apt to pay for your kind of music, so now you have to let them know what you can do.

You should think of selling your music as an information service to potential clients. You're informing them that the music they *need* is available . . . from you.

If You Don't Tell Them, Who Will?

Maybe your mother taught you humility. That's a good trait, but not when it comes to selling your music. Now you need to be a little aggressive – not high-pressure, though, and certainly not obnoxious. You'll have to learn to talk about yourself and the merits of your music.

Bear in mind that there are more musicians looking than there are jobs available, and that your competitors may be out there calling on *your* potential clients. There's only one thing to do – sell your talents. Let people know what you can do.

You'll have an edge over other kinds of sales-people, for you'll be touting yourself and your music. Who knows your abilities better than you? If you know, absolutely, that you can do the job, you'll demonstrate the confidence that will help you sell.

Your Public-Relations Tools

To do an effective job of selling your music, you should be prepared with a few well-produced printed aids. These need not be expensive. If you're artistically inclined, you can design them yourself and have them reproduced at a local copy shop.

Avoid any stock illustrations your printer may have on hand. Instead, commission a commercial artist to design a logo or illustration for your card and other stationery. Some commercial art students do excellent work at low prices, but be sure to look at samples of similar work. Avoid clutter. Aim for a simple, memorable design. Almost everything about music is graphically interesting, and a good artist can use such elements as the staff, notes, keyboard or instrument shapes to develop a design that you will use for years. And it will be yours alone. Here are the PR tools you'll need.

Business cards. Every musician must have business cards. Since these represent you to potential clients, be sure your cards are well done. Use good-quality stock, a clearly legible typeface, and a simple design that matches your style.

You should have a separate card for different facets of your music; one for teaching, one for your band, and a different card entirely for your solo concert work. Trite phrases such as 'Music for all occasions' probably won't help, and might even harm.

One enterprising salesman throws handfuls of his cards into the air at football games. Although you probably won't need to be quite *that* enterprising, you'll want everyone who could need your music to have a card. Always carry a good supply. Many business-people keep business-card files, so clip a card to all your correspondence.

Brochures, flyers, information sheets. Most freelancers need at least one brochure, flyer or information sheet. These can be as simple as a single piece of paper with a *neatly typed* description of what you can do. *Be sure your grammar, usage, and spelling are correct*; mistakes can be distracting, and look unprofessional. An offset printer can turn your clean, camera-ready copy into inexpensive but useful publicity pieces. Your printer can show you how a single sheet can be folded to form a brochure or flyer, and he or she will gladly refer you to artists and typesetters if you need them.

Your printed aids should state, simply:

- who you are
- what you do
- where you have worked, and for whom
- how your music will enhance specific kinds of events
- what others have said about your work – keep copies of good reviews and letters, and use them in preparing sales aids

Be positive and creative, but stick to the truth. If you've never been to Los Angeles, don't bill yourself as 'just back from Los Angeles.' Lies can lead to big trouble.

Photographs. All musicians should have a supply of good, up-to-date 8″ × 10″ photos. Black-and-white pictures are usually fine; colour costs a lot more. Get a good photo and use a printer to make copies and add your name at the bottom.

Audio/video tapes. Some musicians will profit from the use of audio or video demonstration tapes. If you record your music, make sure that the tapes are representative of your talent and appropriate to the client's needs. Make sure, too, that they are very well produced.

Almost everyone has a good sound system at home or at the office – maybe one in the car. Your potential client, through media exposure, has been trained to expect professional-sounding music, even in soap commercials. Be positive that your tape at least approaches this quality. In other words, don't make demo tapes with a £20 cassette player and a built-in microphone.

Feature Yourself

Newspaper, magazine, and radio and television writers in your area, believe it or not, are on constant look-out for interesting material for feature stories. You should try to get valuable publicity for yourself or your group by letting them know anything unusual about your musical activities. Writers on daily papers and reporters for local TV news shows have to fill their space or time every day, so if you're doing something out-of-the-ordinary with your music – and you should be – you should let them know about it.

Think creatively. Is what you are doing – or are about to do – good story material? What's the attention grabber? Does it have broad appeal? Is it interesting – to non-musicians? Pass your ideas to the entertainment or feature editors in your area.

Why do you need publicity? You are building a career in an increasingly competitive profession, and your name should – really *must* – become widely known. When people think of the most outstanding piano teacher, dance band or folk singer in your community, they should think of *you*. Continuing publicity is part of building name recognition. Think of publicity as free advertising, and always be aware of how your musical activities could interest others. Here are a few ideas for feature stories:

- Announcements of recitals, concerts or musical programmes can be turned into feature stories if something uncommon or special is included. You might, say, relate your recital to your town's history by performing the work of a local composer. Perhaps your brass band has won the last 10 band festivals, and you are trying for a record-breaking eleventh. Advise the feature writers in your area, and also notify all the compilers of the events diaries that appear in newspapers and on radio and TV.
- Have you played for so many high-society dances and débutante balls that you've become an indispensable part of the social scene? A profile about you in a local paper could make interesting reading – and create valuable publicity for you.
- Reviews in newspaper entertainment sections offer another way for you to let the public know what you are doing. Often, these reviews cover all the entertainment in an area, so let editorial reviewers know where you are performing and ask to be reviewed. It will help if you provide good quality, black-and-white photos to be run with any reviews.
- Anything unusual or especially noteworthy can be material for a news or feature story. Are you trying to get in the *Guinness Book of Records* by playing the accordion non-stop for two weeks? Did you narrowly escape death when you forgot to check the polarity on your amplifiers and were severely shocked at an outdoor concert? Have you organised a fund-raising event for hungry people in your community? Have you played the piano in the same restaurant for 25 years? Did you accidentally drop your Steinberger bass from a sixth-floor balcony – but not even knock it out of tune? Do you have an impressive collection of antique wind instruments?

So, think creatively and present your ideas in such a way that the writer or editor you approach will see the broad appeal of your ideas. Don't forget that writers and editors *need* stories every day, week or month. Help them find interesting material by telling them about your musical achievements and music-related experiences.

Once a story has appeared about you and your music, be sure that you use it to further your career. You can add impressive quotations to your publicity material or enclose photocopies of the story with your brochure when you do mailings.

If a TV piece has been done on you, be sure to get a videotape copy, and let prospective clients know of its availability.

Sales Basics for Musicians

There are many excellent books on salesmanship in your local library or bookshop, and it will be worth your while to learn from master salesmen. The following basic principles, however, will get you started.

Plan your approach. Before your first sales call to a prospective client, think in detail about what you have to offer. Know *exactly* what you want to sell, what you can do, and how much you expect to be paid. Work on variations of your basic idea, write these ideas down and read over them until you know them well. Many sales-people write such information on three-by-five-inch index cards. They arrange and rearrange the cards to get the best sequence for each presentation.

Practice your sales pitch on your spouse or friends. Have them ask you hard questions. The client will.

If you know in advance what kind of music the client will need, write out a specific proposal before your sales call. Leave a copy with the prospect, and, needless to say, keep a copy for your files. Specify what you are offering, for how long, and how much it will cost.

Make an appointment. Never drop in on a prospect. Assume that your potential clients are busy and that their time is valuable. You must follow standard business practices when dealing with business-people, so call ahead for an appointment.

Ask for your prospect by name whenever possible. If you know only the company name, use your experience and common sense to reach the music buyer. If you are calling on a hotel, for example, you'll probably need the catering or sales department. In a large company, you'll probably deal with the public relations staff.

If you know the event you'd like to talk about, simply ask the operator to connect you with the person in charge of that project, whether it's a Christmas party or an annual company meeting. With good telephone manners and friendly persistence, you can usually reach the right person. Get the proper spelling of your contact's name, and note whether it's 'Miss,' 'Mrs.,' or 'Ms.'

Be punctual. When you have an appointment, be on time or a few minutes early. Whatever you do, don't be late. Allow for rush-hour traffic and parking problems.

Many business-people are suspicious of musicians and artists. When you call on them, you must show that you can abide by their rules. Punctuality is crucial. Why should a client believe that your band will start on time if you're late for your initial meeting?

Be appropriately dressed. Use your client's style as a guide. Don't flaunt your independence from business conventions by dressing too casually; it will set the wrong tone for your meeting.

Be neat and clean. It may seem like stating the obvious, but clean nails, neat hair and fresh breath are important.

Talk about your potential client's musical needs. Ask questions and really listen to the answers.

Try to avoid the word *I* as much as possible. Emphasise *you*, because that's what your client is ultimately interested in – what he wants, what you can do for him. (Your prospective client, of course, could as well be a woman.)

Assess what kind of music is needed and make suggestions that would fulfil these requirements. Show him, in detail, how your music will do what he wants. Emphasise that you'll make him look good to his boss.

Be honest. If a prospect needs something that you can't provide, you'd best tell him so. Never book a job you can't perform well just because you need the money. Both you and your client will lose, and bad news travels fast.

Use supporting material. Give him your brochure. Show him your videotape. Tell him about other clients you've successfully worked for. Give him references (but be sure they're willing to be called on as such). Let him read a few good thank-you letters from satisfied clients.

State your price. Tell him confidently, not apologetically, what you charge. To speak with self-assurance in stating your price, you must determine beforehand the monetary worth of the job you are proposing and be prepared to fill out a contract form. Don't be timid. Be ready to talk about money – that's what business-people deal with every day. (The next chapter goes into detail about pricing your services and preparing contracts.)

Take the initiative. When you've told him what you can do for him, ask for a commitment. Don't be vague or wishy-washy. Don't be embarrassed to talk about money; he knows music isn't free.

If you know you can provide what he needs, take out a contract form and say "Now, shall we get the specifics down in writing so I can hold this date for you?"

Don't prolong the meeting. When you've finished your presentation, leave. No further sales pitch is wanted after you've got a 'yes,' 'no' or 'not at this time.' Don't overstay your welcome, and don't be *too* aggressive. A good relationship can be more valuable than any single sale.

Follow Up

Write it down. Immediately after leaving a prospect's office, write down all the important details you discussed. *Don't trust your memory.* If you need to contact the client or prospect in the future, write a reminder on your calendar or put one in your memo file.

Send a note of appreciation. Write a short thank-you note to each prospect you see, whether he buys music from you or not. If he bought, send a contract with the note. If he didn't, write the note anyway. He'll have a more positive impression if you show your appreciation.

Continue to follow up. Keep in touch with potential clients whether they are business-people, agents or other musicians. Buyers get in ruts, too, and you need to remind them of your availability.

But don't be a pest. An occasional phone call, mailed brochure, or short sales call will keep your name before good prospects. Easy, but regular, does it.

People Need Music

Remember that every client is concerned with his or her needs. We all are self-centred, and your clients aren't necessarily altruists. They want their money's worth.

People don't *require* music the way they need food or shelter, so keep in mind that you are selling a luxury. Thus, you must emphasise what your music can do for prospective clients and show how it will help them in some way. Appeal to their egos and pride as well as their other reasons for buying good music.

Be ready to prove to your potential clients that not only do they need music – they need *your* music. Practise making your selling points in advance so that your sales calls will be enthusiastic and convincing. Here are a few ideas about what music can do. You'll think of more.

Music creates an appropriate atmosphere. Music can be sophisticated, exciting, sedate, lively, contemporary, country, ethnic, celebratory, cultured – you name it. It can set the pace of an event and establish the tone of a gathering.

Live music demonstrates affluence. If your client can afford to have a dance band at a garden party, the guests will be impressed. Sometimes, music is a status symbol.

Music makes an event memorable. For a wedding reception, sales meeting, cocktail function, grand opening, or whatever, music can turn an ordinary party into an event. The photographs of Uncle Albert dancing with all the young girls will be family treasures for years.

Music entertains. The right soloist or group will turn another routine company dinner into a great evening.

Music breaks the ice, encourages mixing, mingling and talking. If your client's sales-people are dancing with potential customers in a hospitality suite, you can bet you have a happy client.

Music brings people together by bridging differences of culture, background and generation.

Music sells. Television jingles may cost tens of thousands of pounds to produce – for only thirty or sixty seconds of music. Why pay that much? Because memorable melodies sell.

Music makes people feel good. If your clients and their guests end up doing the twist, they're probably happy.

Music attracts crowds. A big band in a shopping mall quickly creates a sensation.

Music recalls nostalgic memories. It recreates times past. Your clients will enjoy saying, "They played that when I was in college."

Music helps and heals. Therapists know that music has powers to soothe and calm.

Music even helps people fall in love.

Clients Need Your Music

Even after you convince your prospect that music is essential, your work still isn't over. You've got to convince her or him to hire *you*. Once again, be prepared with as many persuasive reasons as possible why your group is exactly what is needed.

Use the Personal Sales Ideas Worksheet at the end of this chapter to collect your own best selling points. Here are a few suggestions. You should think of more that fit your particular situation, and know them so well that you can answer any objection.

- You're professional. This is what you do for a living, and you provide better quality than part-timers can produce.
- Or, if you're a part-time player, you could argue that you aren't a jaded, bored professional. Point out that you play because you love music, and that your enthusiasm and energy will make up for any lack of professional expertise.
- Repeat that you understand the client's needs well and can provide exactly that kind of music. Give examples to prove your point.
- Remind the prospect that you've played dozens, or hundreds, of similar engagements. You might even say something like, "I'll bet your boss will love us."
- Explain that your equipment is the best, and that the quality of your music is therefore better than the competition's. Offer to let the client use your state-of-the-art sound system for speeches, toasts, or whatever, thus saving the cost of hiring another public-address unit.
- Underline that your band will be not just on time, but early. Tell the client that you will set up your equipment before the party if necessary.
- Show how low your price really is when divided by the number of guests, or in comparison with the total price of the event. Sometimes a wedding cake costs as much as a small combo – even though the band is much more important to the success of the reception.
- If the job you're going after requires virtuosity, expound on your virtuosity – if you possess it. If variety is the key, explain that you can play the full spectrum that will be needed – if you can. (Don't exaggerate your abilities. If you don't perform up to expectations, you will be in the hot seat – and will lose the client.)
- If you can, present letters of recommendation resulting from similar jobs, and offer a list of current and former clients that you know will vouch for your music. Again, word of mouth has very strong persuasive power.

If you prepare and make well-thought-out sales presentations, your prospects will realise that you can, indeed, help them. Then they will no longer be prospects. They will be clients.

PERSONAL SALES IDEAS WORKSHEET

What My Music Can Do _____

What's Best about My Music _____

What Others Have Liked about My Music _____

Why My Music is a Bargain _____

Why I'm Better than My Competition _____

CHAPTER SIXTEEN

PRICING AND CONTRACTS

As you locate clients who are willing to pay you to perform, it's essential that you know how much your music is worth to them – and also to you.

Then, once price and other details have been settled, you need to send contracts or letters of confirmation.

These details are sometimes tiresome, even boring. But they are crucial nonetheless.

How Much Should You Charge? How Much Are You Worth?

Make the price right. Try to price your music just above the average for your community. If you quote too low, your client will be suspicious and won't respect you. And your colleagues will be hostile if they learn that you undercut the norm. If you price yourself too high, however, you'll lose sales.

How do you know what to charge for your music? This is a difficult question, and you'll find that there will be a good bit of variation as you sell.

Find out what your competitors charge by calling them (or getting a friend to do it) and getting their price for a particular kind of job. Keep a list of what other musicians and agents request for certain musical services. Remember, too, that many variables influence the price; you'll charge more in December than in July, more on Saturday night than Tuesday afternoon, more for driving 60 miles than driving six streets, more if equipment must be carried up two flights of steps, and more to ICI than to a bride's father.

Know, ultimately, what it's worth to you, and stick to it. If the going price for a three-hour solo piano job in your area is £125, know in advance whether you'd play it for £100. Or £75. You'll need to be flexible, but it's very important to stick to your standards. Business clients expect it, they wouldn't sell their services at half price and neither should you.

If you have an exclusive, a really special act, you should obviously ask for more money.

Remember that many large companies expect to spend lots of money. Think in their terms, not yours.

If you have to cut your price, try to cut your proposal a corresponding amount. That is, you could drop an instrument or cut an hour from the total to justify a price reduction.

Here are more suggestions for pricing your music.

Join the Musician's Union. Membership offers several advantages. One is the *union scale,* which should be your *minimum* charge. Usually, the scale is a complex system of charges, based on the kind of job involved, the purpose of the music, length of job, number of musicians, and so on. Sometimes, the suggested rate is too low for your talent and your market. In that case, raise your price. At other times, the scale will keep the price up, and you'll be glad you're a member of the union.

When you get involved in recording work – jingles, demos, industrial film scores, for example – you'll find that the union scale can be very important. A union may keep close watch on studios and recording clients, and often residual payments continue to come in long after the recording is finished. These are payments that the client makes each time your recorded music is used. In such cases, payment is fixed by the union, and its rules and regulations must be strictly followed.

Remember that agency profits and expenses must be added to your fees. You may decide to take a little less when booking through an agency. In return, however, you should expect the agency to take care of such business details as contracts and billing.

On the other hand, when you book directly, your price should be competitive with agency charges. In other words, don't undercut the agents, or they'll stop using you.

Never perform free of charge unless it is for a very good cause and you are philanthropically contributing your time and talent. Only amateurs play 'for exposure,' and such exposure is almost always non-existent and thus worthless. If you play without a fee, you are likely to be taken advantage of.

If you are asked to contribute your time and music to a legitimate charity or fund-raising event, think carefully before you donate your music. It's likely that other participants are being paid – the caterer, florist and photographer, for example – and you should be no different. Often, legitimate fund-raising events have considerable production budgets, and the money is raised from those who pay to attend, not from those who perform. If you do perform gratis, you should get a letter from the sponsor thanking you for your specific donation so that you can at least claim a tax deduction.

This is not an unfriendly, unfeeling approach to charities. There are so many good causes that you could give your music away every day. Unfortunately, that won't help pay the rent.

Make a chart listing all your prices for various sized groups and different kinds of jobs. Then you'll be able to quote prices promptly when talking to different clients. Devising such a chart isn't easy, because you need to be consistent and fair to yourself while not charging too much or too little. Should a three-hour job cost the client three times as much as a one-hour job? Should overtime simply be pro-rated, or should your overtime rate be a little higher to compensate for unexpected changes in your schedule?

Incidentally, you'll probably discover that the more you charge, the more you are respected. Interestingly, the opposite is usually true, too. The less you charge, the poorer your reputation – not to mention your wallet.

Don't forget to include any extras the union or 'local custom' adds. There is probably a standard extra fee for rehearsal time and for shows. But what about carrying charges for heavy, hard-to-move instruments such as pianos, drum kits, harps and organs?

Often, too, you must add 'doubling fees' for players who provide and play more than one instrument. A reed player who doubles on flute, clarinet and two or three different saxes will make considerably more money than the trombone player who plays only his or her primary instrument. These factors are very important on large jobs. Make sure that *all* the important fees are included when you quote a price.

Television and videotaping have other, usually higher, scales and sometimes present pitfalls to unwary musicians. More than one band has walked out when the client started videotaping a stage show or business meeting without paying the appropriate rate. Be sure you and your musicians will be paid for your music if the client decides to make a training film or videotape of your performance. And be sure this is understood in advance.

One singer, making a videotape for her own sales use, was stunned that the 12-piece band backing her show insisted on an extra payment of more than £25 per player to permit her to videotape the proceedings. She had thought the musicians would be happy to help her produce a videotape that would sell the show *and* their backing music. The band members, however, didn't agree, and they refused to play without assurances that their extra demands would be met.

Charge what the market will bear. As you work more, and are more and more in demand, you'll probably want to follow the basic free-market pricing strategy and charge what you can get. If you are the best, or only band of your kind in town, you may be able to raise your price accordingly. Be careful, however, not to disregard your community's norms, or you may price yourself out of the market. And obviously, when you charge more, you should provide more variety and better-quality entertainment for the client's money.

Get It In Writing

Once you and your client have agreed on the details of the job and you have been hired, it's time to send a contract. There are two very important reasons why you should *always have a contract or letter of confirmation*:

1. Writing down the details in black and white reduces the chances of a misunderstanding. Spell out the time of day and the date. There is always room for error, but if you have a signed contract hiring you for seven o'clock on Tuesday, May 12, your client can't claim that you should have been there at six o'clock on Monday, May 11. This is not a far-fetched example; such mistakes happen every day.

2. If the worst should happen, and your client won't pay you, a signed contract will be crucial when you go to the union, or to court, to claim your money.

What Should a Contract Include?

What form should your contract take? What points should it cover? This book does not offer legal advice, and if you need a cast-iron contract you should probably consult a lawyer. However, for most situations, that won't be necessary, and clarity is what you're after. Here are some considerations:

- If you are in the Musicians' Union, use its standard contract form. It is widely recognised, covers the important points clearly, and protects you as much as possible.
- If you aren't a union member or if you'd prefer to devise your own contract or confirmation letter, be sure that it includes all the necessary information. Standard practice is to send two signed copies to the client – one for him or her, and one to be returned, signed, to you.

One good idea is to have your own contract form printed on your letterhead and include clauses pertinent to you. This personalises the contract, makes you seem more professional, and saves you time. If you decide to create your own standard form, be sure to include:

- Today's date
- Name, address, telephone number and title of the client
- Definition of the band or group – size and instrumentation
- Fee agreed on, and when payment will be made
- Overtime charges, if necessary
- Deposit required, if any, and conditions for refunding it
- Appropriate dress for the job
- Special requirements or requests

In addition, you may wish to include pre-printed 'conditions' clauses that will be applicable to all your jobs. Unexpected circumstances can cause real problems, and you'll avoid confusion if you decide, *in advance,* what to do. Here are a few ideas you may find useful.

- What if the affair is cancelled? The wedding is called off, there's a death in the family, or the couple starts divorce proceedings a week before their anniversary party. Will you return the deposit, or is it (as it usually is) non-refundable?
- What if bad weather causes a last-minute change? Snowstorms or heavy rain can play havoc with plans. If extremely bad weather is remotely possible in your area, make provisions for it in your contract.
- What if a sudden rain-storm forces the garden party to move indoors with only one hour remaining? You may wish to add an extra set-up fee or carriage charge to compensate for the unpleasant task of moving unexpectedly during a job.

  Or perhaps the client just forgot to tell you that the cocktail hour will be by the pool, the dinner will be up two flights of stairs on the deck, and the dance will be in the ballroom. If you've written in an extra fee for any location moves, you'll feel better as you drag your set of drums up and down all those steps.
- If the client is providing an instrument for you to play – usually a piano – specify that it be in reasonable tune and in good working order. Or require that it must be tuned prior to your performance. Add a carriage fee for bringing your own equipment to the job in case theirs isn't playable when you arrive.

- You may wish to add an extra fee for early set-up time or a consulting fee for extra meetings with the clients. What if the host of a house party wants you to drive 40 miles out to 'look over' the room where you'll be playing? Will you charge for the extra trip? What if the bride and groom want to have a two-hour meeting to discuss the music for their two-hour reception? Will you charge for your time?
- What if you have to buy special music and spend time transposing and learning it for a wedding ceremony? You may have to buy a £10 book you'll never use again to find one obscure tune. Will you pass this charge on to the client?

If you simply spell out these items as stipulations in your standard contract form and note that they apply to all jobs, you'll save many headaches and much confusion. Usually, just deciding in advance what to do will ensure that the engagement goes smoothly.

Maybe your kind of music doesn't require so much detail, or maybe you don't work that many jobs. In these cases, a simple letter to your client will probably suffice, but be sure to include any pertinent details mentioned above. Use your letterhead and be simple and direct. There's an example on the page opposite.

Obviously, you'd save time by using a standard contract form and not having to write a complete letter to each client. Also, if you use a form, you won't be as likely to overlook any important points.

In any case, whether you get a lawyer to help you devise a contract or just write a confirmation letter like the sample included here, be sure you get a written agreement. Everything will go better if you do, and you might be sorry if you don't.

17 September, 1990

John Davies, Esq.
123 Willow Drive
Henley-on-Thames
OXON

Dear Mr. Davies,

This letter will confirm our engagement to provide music for your son's 21st birthday party to be held on Saturday, October 12, 1990, from 9.00pm until 2.00am at Henley Boat Club. My band, 'The Mellowtones,' consists of five pieces plus a female vocalist, and will be dressed formally.

As we discussed on the phone, we will provide our own sound system but will use the house piano. You have assured me that the piano will be in good tune and placed on the stage by 7.00pm that evening.

Our fee for this engagement is £750, to be paid to me at the end of the evening. If overtime is required, the rate is £100 per *half hour*.

Please let me know in advance if there are any special requests.

One copy of this letter is for your file, and the second copy should be signed and returned to me.

Thank you for booking us. We very much look forward to the engagement.

Yours sincerely,

Joe Jones,
Band-leader

Accepted by _____

(Address)
_____

(Telephone)
_____

CHAPTER SEVENTEEN

PLAYING THE JOB

Now you've booked a job – or dozens of them. The hardest part of the freelance music business, finding work, is behind you. Your next concern is that the job itself goes well.

For one thing, you'd like to work again for this client. For another, your reputation as 'the musician to call' is built one job at a time. What makes a memorable job and a happy client? What makes a job go over well?

Part of the answer has little to do with music. In fact, *the success of a job often depends on non-musical factors.* It's not just how (or what) you play. It may be whether your shoes are polished or whether you start on time. Little things mean a lot, and the values of the business world don't parallel those of many musicians.

Do's and Don'ts For Every Job

Here are some recommendations that apply to all freelance music jobs. While they won't guarantee success, they'll get you started.

Know what you're supposed to do. This isn't as easy as it sounds. Be sure you understand what the client wants. When she says she wants old-style music, does she mean Beethoven or Cole Porter? Or does she mean anything soft and slow and written before 1950? Some clients are musically naive, so be careful to define terms.

Vagueness always causes trouble. If your client wants jazz, that could mean swing or fusion, Louis Armstrong or Wynton Marsalis. Clear communication and definition of terms solve this problem. It can be helpful to get specific suggestions from the client to find out what he really has in mind.

Try to determine the client's *intangible* and *indefinite* needs. Is he trying to hire a band that will please his boss? Is he trying to impress his guests with his sophistication? Or does he want a rowdy, good-time atmosphere? If you can accurately assess your client's needs, *stated or not*, you'll have a much better chance of fulfilling them.

Communicate during the job. Check periodically with your client to be sure that everything is going well. Sometimes she won't complain until it's too late, or for some reason she may feel awkward about interrupting your performance to request a change.

Your selection of tunes, stage demeanour, volume, lighting, tempo and so on can be changed if necessary. Remember, in commercial situations you're hired to fulfil a particular need, not necessarily to express yourself musically.

A cliché is appropriate here: the boss may not always be right, but he's always the boss. If your client wants to hear 'New York, New York' again (for the fifth time), play it again. Grit your teeth and bear it, think about the money you'll make from that tune, or play it in a different key for practice.

Try to avoid the musician-client hostility that sometimes develops. The easiest way to keep everyone happy is to keep talking. Communicate with your client.

Details are crucial. To repeat, the quality of the music doesn't always determine the success of a job. Often it's the little things, the insignificant details so easy to overlook, that the client will remember.

So be early to the job. Check the lighting, the sound, the piano, the location of the service lift, parking, whether the electrical supply works, where you can store your equipment cases, and where the dressing rooms are.

Make sure that the house lights won't be turned off just when you start reading the most important music of the evening, and be certain that turning off the house lights won't also turn off your electricity.

Find out if the musicians are invited to eat and drink with the guests, who authorises overtime, what the boss's favourite song is, what the newly-weds' first dance will be.

Don't forget to double-check with musicians you have hired about time, place, instruments needed, doublings, rehearsals, proper dress and pay. Remember to have extra music-stand light bulbs, guitar cords, bow ties and whatever else is most likely to break or be forgotten.

It is unfortunate, but even though your music is perfectly chosen and performed, the client may remember only that you started 10 minutes late or that the sax player wore a blue shirt instead of white.

The music must be right and as good as possible, but don't overlook all those little, but important, details.

Keep it all under control. When you are asked to do the impossible, don't be hostile. The client, or audience, probably doesn't understand the technical reasons why your trio can't sound like Michael Jackson's latest hit. Don't try to explain by talking about overdubs, studio musicians, backing singers, and so on; the client will probably think you are just making excuses. It's easier to explain politely that you don't know the requested song and suggest something similar that you *can* do. Nobody knows everything (except teenage audiences).

One way to stay in control is to have the next tune always in mind. Wasting time between numbers will make your audience restless and give people time to think up hundreds of requests that you can't do.

Always tune instruments, replace broken strings, and test microphones *before* the job begins. Nothing is as irritating to people enjoying a quiet dinner, for example, as loud guitar tuning or repeated "Testing, 1, 2, 3 . . . " Of course tuning and testing are crucial, but do them early, before the job begins.

Follow up. Write a short thank-you note to the client after the job (unless it was booked through an agency). Let her know that you appreciate her business and that you'd like to work for her again. Enclose your card. If you're sending an invoice, a thank-you note will soften its impact. In any case, the extra few minutes spent following up will be appreciated.

Your client has no doubt paid you a considerable sum of money. Don't vanish without a trace. You'll need her again.

Maintain enthusiasm. A professional level of competence is certainly important to your success as a freelance musician, but so is your attitude, your demeanour while playing for money. There are lots of excellent musicians who barely make a living, while many less-proficient players make much more money. Why should this be so?

If you regard playing music commercially as a chore, your attitude will inevitably be communicated to your listeners, and they'll resent it. If you're taking their money, they can rightly expect your cheerful best.

If you're bored with a particular job or tired, don't show it. Try to show enthusiasm instead. This can be hard to do, but it's worth the effort.

Consider yourself fortunate, as a freelance musician, to be paid for doing what you most enjoy. Play each job as though you welcome the opportunity. You might make more money in another profession, but you'd miss the excitement and the joy of music.

CHAPTER EIGHTEEN

THE SUCCESSFUL FREELANCE MUSICIAN

Some freelance musicians always seem to do well, constantly working and in demand. Other, perhaps more talented players sit at home and watch TV. What determines success? How can you continue to expand the demand for your music? Here are some suggestions.

Practise, Practise, Practise!

Like a doctor or lawyer, musicians *practise* their profession. You'll never know everything about music, and you'll never reach perfection. But you'll certainly be better off by working at it.

One way to keep yourself fresh and ensure demand for your music is to continue to practise. Learn new tunes, master current styles. Try not to become so identified with one type of music that your career depends on its continued popularity. You probably won't like every new musical fad, but if you understand and can play the 'latest' well, you'll be in a better position to market your skills. That's because you'll have more skills to market.

Playing music is like athletic ability: use it or lose it. Practise is the way to win in the freelance music competition . . . and keep on winning.

Keep Up to Date

Keep up with changes in the broad music world. How will synthesisers affect what you do? Computers? Electronics? You can't hide your head and hope that new trends and technologies will go away. They simply won't.

Do you like music video? Hate it? It doesn't really matter how you feel about it because it's here and will remain part of the music world. We all have to learn how to cope with what's happening.

We can reduce the stress caused by rapid change by trying not to judge until we understand. Remember all those musicians who said rock music wouldn't last? And remember all those rock musicians who said their music would obliterate everything else?

New markets appear, new technologies develop, new kinds of music are created, or old ones are resurrected. If you keep up, you'll be happier and more successful. If you rigidly refuse to watch what's happening, you'll be frustrated – and left behind.

One way to stay in tune is by reading in your field. There are many excellent magazines that cover specific areas of music, and you will profit from reading them. You won't find all of these magazines at your local newsagent; you may have to subscribe, but the cost of professional magazines and journals is tax deductible.

Some Ideas About Money

It's hard to be happy, or feel successful, when you're worried about the rent. Freelance musicians, with no steady work and with erratic income, are good prospects for money-caused ulcers. Here are a few ways to counter this ever-present problem.

Save money. Saving money may not be easy to do, but nothing is more important for your peace of mind. Figure out some way to put money aside. Ask your bank manager for advice. To start, save any unexpected income; don't spend that £50 from the last-minute job you played on Friday night. Since you weren't counting on it, save it.

You'll be able to relax when you have a growing savings plan, and you'll then be able to borrow more readily if you have to.

Every freelancer needs a cushion, a safety net. You'll have to provide your own, and saving is the best way to start

Join a pension scheme. This is really planning for the future – for the day when either you are physically unable to continue a full-time schedule of playing music or you choose active retirement. You'll also gain a sense of accomplishment and direction if you know you are getting ahead financially.

Know when to stop buying equipment. Don't spend all your money on musical equipment. Face it, there will *always* be something you *absolutely* need, but you'd have to be rich to keep up with the glittering inventory of a music shop. Don't let the marketing wizards manipulate you into unmanageable debt. The latest synthesiser won't necessarily help your playing, nor will a new mouthpiece give you the ultimately perfect sound.

Resist the temptation to be a world-class consumer.

Don't Stop

As your career grows, you'll probably find that you are increasingly in demand. People will know you, and you won't have to work as hard to find jobs. Don't stop now. You can't quit marketing your talents.

Keep adding to your PMMS as you acquire new skills and discover job possibilities. Continue to call on new clients and reinforce your relationship with old ones.

Remember, *if you're coasting, you're going downhill*. When you become successful, someone will always be poised to take your place.

One More Time

The productive freelance music life can be wonderful. You can do what you enjoy – and get paid for it.

You can work in a variety of situations, each with new challenges and opportunities for success. You won't be limited by bureaucratic rules. You can get to know many interesting people and become well-known in your community. You might even make more money from your enjoyable work than you ever considered possible.

You can succeed in the freelance music business if you work hard and don't stop. To an extent exciting to think about, you'll be in control of your own future.

I hope that the marketing methods described here will work as well for you as they have for me. If you use them, I'm sure you'll succeed.

Good luck?

INDEX